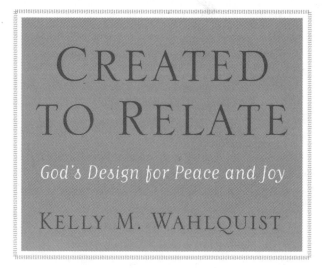

CREATED TO RELATE

God's Design for Peace and Joy

KELLY M. WAHLQUIST

servant

AN IMPRINT OF
FRANCISCAN MEDIA
Cincinnati, Ohio

Scripture passages have been taken from the *Revised Standard Version*, Catholic edition. Copyright 1946, 1952, 1971 by the Division of Christian Education of the National Council of Churches of Christ in the USA. Used by permission. All rights reserved. Quotes are taken from the English translation of the *Catechism of the Catholic Church* for the United States of America (indicated as *CCC*), 2nd ed. Copyright 1997 by United States Catholic Conference—Libreria Editrice Vaticana.

Cover design by Mary Ann Smith
Cover image © Masterfile
Book design by Mark Sullivan

LIBRARY OF CONGRESS CATALOGING-IN-PUBLICATION DATA
Wahlquist, Kelly M.
Created to relate : God's design for peace and joy / Kelly M. Wahlquist.
pages cm
Includes bibliographical references and index.
ISBN 978-1-61636-876-0 (alk. paper)
1. Interpersonal relations—Religious aspects—Christianity. 2. Women—Psychology. I. Title.
BV4597.52.W34 2015
248.4—dc23
2014042831

ISBN: 978-1-61636-876-0

Published by Servant Books, an imprint of Franciscan Media.
28 W. Liberty St.
Cincinnati, OH 45202
www.FranciscanMedia.org

Printed in the United States of America.
Printed on acid-free paper.
16 17 18 19 20 5 4 3 2

CONTENTS

FOREWORD
Jeff Cavins

All of life is relational. We were not created to be alone!

Throughout the entire Bible we see one person after another relating either well or poorly with one another or with God. Adam tells us that his misfortune was due to his relationship with the woman that God gave him. Cain asks the question, "Am I my brother's keeper?" Young David wants to know the reward for killing the giant Philistine, Goliath, and it ends up becoming a new relationship, Saul's daughter Michal. The reward entails a whole new group of relationships that could either end in joy or sorrow.

Throughout the Bible we see that the key to victory and fruitfulness is very much tied to relationship, both with God and one another. In fact, if you were to condense the Bible down to one description, you could say that it's all about how you and God relate and how you and your neighbor relate.

We see that the gray-haired elders relate to the young and pass on to them wisdom and insight. The wealthy relate to the poor by donating their field to the disadvantaged in hopes they will glean what others have left behind. The widow benefits from her relationship with the broader community, which helps to ease the suffering that results from having lost her husband.

The strong can benefit the weak, and the weak can benefit everyone by offering up their suffering. Paul said, "I rejoice in my sufferings for your sake..." (Colossians 1:24). Paul uses the analogy of the body and the various parts working with one another to describe the beauty and the power of the body of Christ. Even the Church is described as a living temple built with stones, one placed upon another (see 1 Peter 2:5).

Because we are united to Christ, we enjoy a profound unity with one another. The flip side is that we don't have the luxury of being united to Christ while remaining independent of one another. The fact that some in the body of Christ have died physically and gone on to be with the Lord does not separate them from his body. Even in death, we relate to one another. Even if we sin and choose to not physically interact with the body of Christ, St. John Paul II tells us that our sin has a ripple effect on one another. Because sin is familial, it affects not only your relationship with God, but also his entire family. While sin is committed personally, it is perpetuated in community, which makes sin easier to commit as each generation passes.

There is no sin, not even the most intimate and secret one, the most strictly individual one, that exclusively concerns the person committing it. Every sin has repercussions on the entire ecclesial body and the whole human family.[1]

If we are created for relationship and family, why do we see so much pain and strife in the relationships between friends, families, and countries? St. John Paul II tells us that the "refusal of God's fatherly love and of his loving gifts is always at the root of humanity's divisions."[2]

The question isn't whether we relate; this is a given. Instead we should be asking, "Will we relate well?" We should ask, "Will we hinder God's beautiful family plan?" The human being created in the image and likeness of God is an awesome creation. When you put two of these awesome creations together, life can become complex. We are complex beings who are capable of loving, forgiving, walking in humility, crying out in prayer, standing in faith, sacrificing, and being thankful. We are also capable of over-indulging, shaming one another, living in envy, acting out in anger, hiding in fear, being lonely, and falling into hopelessness.

How we live—whether we grow in virtue or gain victory over the struggles of the heart—depends on our relationship with God and how we manage the complex tapestry we call relationships. They defeat us or give way to victory based on our cooperation with the One who created us.

In sports, it's not the star that matters. A team doesn't win because there is one star. A team wins when they learn to relate to each other and appreciate each other's gifts. This was clearly demonstrated during the 1980 Lake Placid Winter Olympics when the US Olympic hockey team, made up of a bunch of average American players assembled by Herb Brooks, defeated the mighty Soviet Union. When Herb Brooks was asked why he did not choose the best players in America, he responded that he wasn't looking for the best players in America—he was looking for the best team.[3]

Today, God is not assembling an all-star team to do his work in the world; rather, he is building his family into a cohesive, loving movement that will advance his mission.

Jesus said that ultimately the world would determine whether he was sent by God by the way his family related to each other... specifically how we love each other. Jesus said, "A new commandment I give to you, that you love one another; even as I have loved you, that you also love one another. By this all men will know that you are my disciples, if you have love for one another" (John 13:34–35).

Our relationship with God is very much tied to our relationship with other members of his family. At one point Jesus said, "So if you are offering your gift at the altar, and there remember that your brother has something against you, leave your gift there before the altar and go; first be reconciled to your brother, and then come and offer your gift" (Matthew 5:23–24).

Years ago I hired Kelly Wahlquist to work with me in creating Bible study small groups. I noticed that she was very good at relating to people and making them a part of a greater vision. She has a beautiful gift for making people feel loved by God. She also has a gift for noticing other people's strengths and blending those strengths to form great teams. If you read her writings carefully you will see that she understands relationships very well, particularly relationships among women.

Created to Relate will open your eyes to the fact that everyone you meet provides you with a new opportunity. You'll learn how your zeal for the Lord can naturally be combined with the joy of meeting new people—people God loves—and loving them into his kingdom.

If you ever want to learn how life is radically relational...write a book. Though it may be one name that appears in the space reserved for the author, the truth is that no thought, no inkling, no inspiration could end up on paper if it wasn't wrapped in the understanding, compassion, support, nurturing, encouragement, hard work, sacrifice, prayers, and self-giving love of others. For me, that list of others is humbling and at the same time, it causes me to thank God with an overflowing heart of gratitude for the many blessings he has bestowed on my life through the relationships he has given me.

I am very thankful to my husband, Andy, and my three beautiful—and patient—children, Annika, Alannah, and Myles, for letting a MacBook Air take my attention away from them for a time (though their father and I have experienced *their* iPhones/laptops/iPads having the same effect) and for surviving mealtime in a dining room with table that was constantly covered in books.

I am grateful to my mom and dad for their continued support, encouragement, and prayers. They are the ones who first taught me what it means to relate to others with love—to strive to be completely self-giving. And they are the ones who instilled in me a deep love for my Catholic faith by sacrificing so much to make sure I grew up knowing and loving Jesus.

The purpose of this book is to express the importance of the relationships in our lives, and at the same time build better relationships. Therefore, I want to thank the brilliant builders, the ones who helped me to formulate the meditations, questions, and reflections, as well as the practical suggestions on how to improve your relationships with others at the end of each chapter. I am forever grateful to my dear friends Dr. Carol Younger, Carol Marquardt, and Margie Mandli for unselfishly sharing with me their gifts of uniting people through prayer, story, and conversation.

Thank you to my amazing editor, Nancy Jo Sullivan. She has been my "Elizabeth" in so many ways, meeting me in my need, and supporting, motivating, and challenging me along the way. Thank you, too, to those who prayed for me daily, especially my dear sisters in Christ, Sue Thrun and Patti Jannuzzi. Your constant prayers, notes, phone calls, and words of encouragement held me up so many times.

None of this would have been possible had it not been for the beautiful women who have guided me, supported me, and prayed for me all throughout this incredible journey. You know who you are! If I listed all your names, I'm sure it would constitute a whole 'nother book. I'm totally serious—for along with the many of you who are my anchor and support today, there are many in heaven who I know are pulling for me. I worked in a convent for twenty years. (For the record, I was very young when I started working there.) I know I have many holy women standing before the Lord, asking him to shower me with his grace. Sr. Mary John Ryan, I know you are leading the pack.

I especially want to thank my friend and colleague, Jeff Cavins, for opening my heart to a deeper relationship with the Lord by introducing me to a love of Sacred Scripture; for recognizing a gift in me that I didn't know I had; for encouraging me to work in that gift; and for creating an opportunity for me to do so by hiring me to literally "build relationships." This book about relationships is a result of his vision and passion to make disciples for Christ and build the kingdom of God, and his ability to listen and act when he hears the voice of the Lord. I am blessed to be his student.

G.K. Chesterton once said, "Angels can fly because they can take themselves lightly."[4] What a beautiful concept: realizing that it is not us, but God who carries the weight of the world, thus freeing us from the gravitational pull of our own importance.

When I am in the company of great men and women of faith, I am often awestruck by their joyful disposition, contagious passion, and engaging cheerfulness. When I first found myself running in their circles, about a decade ago, I thought that it was merely their incredible humility, their absolute faith that God is so much bigger than them, that allowed them to surrender entirely to his mercy and at the same time do so with a smile. For there truly is a "lightness" to one who knows he or she is nothing and God is everything. Those who believe they are everything seldom wear such a smile of contentment.

What I've grown to learn in ten years of being welcomed and embraced by these wonderful people is that they are constantly striving to completely surrender to the will of God; they are constantly longing for conversion. No matter how holy they appear in my eyes, each of them is seeking to know the Lord in a deeper and more intimate way; each of them is aspiring to know and do the will of the Father. This complete surrender to the will of God is a task that can seem daunting and overwhelming, but much of the lightness (and laughter) of these men and women striving for holiness comes from knowing they are not alone in their journey—they recognize that God has given them relationships to nurture, guide, protect, and encourage them along the way.

My own journey has been one of joy and sorrow, excitement and fear, tremendous accomplishments and thunderous downfalls, but I know that every inch of this path back to the heart of the Father, be it rocky or smooth, is lined with blessings. For me, these blessings are *all* found in relationship. Through each hardship, I have grown in my relationships. Through each trial, I have learned who was there to hold me up, and I've sadly recognized those who would let me fall. Through each success, I have seen the work of those who supported me. And through each and every experience, I have grown deeper in my relationships with my family, with friends, with new acquaintances, and most importantly, with the Lord.

There was a time in my life when I feared I had lost all that was near and dear to me—above all, I feared I had lost dozens of relationships. My heart sank and my stomach literally ached as I envisioned friendships, embedded deep in my heart, coming to a drastic halt. I remember explaining to my mom that I felt as though I had just gone through an excruciatingly painful breakup with a college boyfriend, only amplified. It felt more like I was breaking up with forty people I loved dearly. It was a feeling that left me sick to my stomach and teetering on despair. But what I feared would happen never materialized. Instead, I learn a valuable lesson about the depth of relationships rooted in Christ. I grew closer to all those beautiful people God put in my life, and I developed a new and intimate relationship with the three most important Persons in my life—God the Father, God the Son, and God the Holy Spirit.

The lesson learned during that time of pain was that God, infinitely perfect and blessed in himself has a plan of sheer goodness for my life, and much of his plan involves the relationships he has given to me to nurture, guide, protect, and encourage me along my journey back to him. First and foremost, he has called me into an intimate relationship with him, and he has given me his Son, his Spirit, and the Blessed Mother to guide me. He has also placed people in my path who are with him right now in heaven, and he continues to put people in my life everyday who nurture, teach, love, encourage, and inspire me on this journey.

The purpose of this book is to share what I have learned on this journey with the hope that it will help you—and that is that life is *radically relational.* We have all been created in and for relationship, yet I believe that women—in a special way—have been created specifically to be relational. I would say, women, by their very creation and the gifts bestowed upon them, are truly radically relational. Knowing and understanding this, whether you are a man or a woman, will help you in your own personal relationships, and ultimately assist you on your own spiritual journey.

In the past few years I have been blessed with wonderful relationships, relationships that have drawn me deeper into a relationship with the Lord, and thus ever closer to being able to surrender to the will of the Father. Many of those relationships resulted from time spent traveling to share my love of Sacred Scripture and my passion for evangelization; many of those relationships were formed in the small group setting, where I found fellowship and was supported, nurtured, and encouraged by wonderful women striving just like me. As such, I am always eager to promote such opportunities for others and therefore, I encourage you to use this book in a book club or small group setting.

Each chapter concludes with a section called "Tools For Building Your Relationships." As the most important relationship to build is your relationship with God, I begin with a Scripture to read, meditate, pray, and contemplate. Then, I provide a guided meditation, meant to help you enter into the story and thus deepen your relationship with the Lord. Next, you will find proposed questions for reflection and discussion with others, perhaps in a small group setting—for often our relationships with others reveal our spiritual needs with the Lord. The questions are divided into three categories geared to help you grow in all your relationships:

1. What can we learn from God's Word and from the saints?
2. What does the world in which we live say?
3. How are *you* being called to relate?

Knowing we must be not just hearers of the Word, but also doers, I conclude each week with two suggestions of how you can live out your relational gift. One suggestion is a bit more active than the other. You can choose to do one or both.

It is truly my hope that the stories in these pages, the meager and humble insights, and the beautiful meditations, prayers, and reflections at the end of each chapter will help you in some way take yourself "lightly" and fly to new heights in your relationships—heights you never thought possible...and as you soar, may you come to know the peace of Christ that surpasses all understanding.

PART ONE

Built for Relationship

CHAPTER ONE

Longing for Relationship

"Don't sign up for everything!"

Those were my husband's parting words as I walked out of the house late one August evening on my way to Back-to-School Night. It was crazy, after only ten years of marriage; somehow this man thought I was an easy target for any committee looking for a chairperson, co-chair, secretary, treasurer, go-fer, or just a worker.

Our girls were in first grade and preschool, and I was eagerly on my way to see all the opportunities their small Catholic school had awaiting my skill set. My husband opted to stay behind with our ten-month-old son and avoid any occasions for future volunteering, or so he thought.

After a wonderful presentation by the principal on how working together and giving of our time, talent, and treasure would make these little ones the leaders of tomorrow, leaders driven by faith and virtue, I felt compelled to do my part. Heeding my husband's words, however, I did not sign up for everything. I merely signed up to be a host family at the New Family Meet and Greet, to be on the committees for All Saints Day, Grandparents' Day, and the Epiphany Party, to organize the Parent Social and Mother-Daughter events, to host the St. Valentine's Day party for the first grade class, and to co-chair the big annual Gala and Golf

Tournament…oh, and to oversee the May Crowning. Really, how can you pass up helping children process around a parking lot with wilted flowers picked the night before to honor the Blessed Mother? These all seemed doable, because really, aren't they all in different seasons? (For the record, I did not sign up for the Father-Son Camping and Canoe Trip.)

As I was walking out, proud that I had not really overcommitted, a table set up with color-coded charts, colored pencils, and beautiful binders caught my eye. I slowed down to see what it was, and without hesitation, my friend Nichole, who was running this table, said, "You have to do this! You'll love it!"

I looked at the color-coded chart closer and saw that it outlined certain books of the Bible, showing events in world history that were occurring at the same time. I will admit, I was intrigued, but I didn't want to let on, lest I end up with one more commitment. So, I rather nonchalantly asked, "What is this?"

Nichole enthusiastically responded, "It's a great Bible study! You have to sign up for it!"

I glanced down at The Great Adventure Bible Study. "Are you crazy?" I said. "I can't sign up for one more thing! If I do, my husband will kill me. I can barely commit to flossing my teeth for the two weeks before I go to the dentist—how can I commit to a twenty-four-week Bible study?"

But Nichole pleaded with me. "Please, you have to sign up. If you sign up, everyone will sign up!" She didn't have any takers yet, and I felt badly about declining.

The next morning after scooting two pigtailed girls off to school and cleaning up baby food from the floors and walls from breakfast, I got a phone call. On the other end was my friend Jozy.

"Kelly, we saw you signed up for The Great Adventure Bible Study, so a whole group of us did too—there are forty of us." She began listing names: "Jennie, Carrie, Jody, Liz, Allison, Jane, Tiffany, Kathy, Jo, Pam, Ginny, etc…" until she had named probably all the moms of the students in the school! As I listened to her zeal for this undertaking, the wheels in my head were spinning.

"That's great, Jozy. Let me call you back in a few minutes."

I immediately dialed the phone, and when my friend answered, I said in a long, drawn-out tone, *"Ni…chole?"*

"Please, please, hear me out," she pleaded.

Then she proceeded to make her argument. She knew if I signed up, others would; it was the best Bible study out there; it was taught by an amazing teacher; I wouldn't regret it; reading Scripture would bring me closer to Jesus… In her last ditch effort to convince me to stay in the group, Nichole said three golden words: "Free child care."

The last five years of my life had been consumed with conversations with children. I had spent ample time explaining to a crying four-year-old that Barbie was going to be OK, and that it was just easier for Grandpa to get her dress on if he took her head off, and once he had the outfit on, he'd put the head back on her; then she and Ken could happily ride in her convertible all over the living room floor. My days were filled with talk about Teletubbies and Dora the Explorer, or trying to coax a child into eating vegetables and drinking milk, listing every reason under the sun why they were better for her than Skittles and Juicy Juice. My evenings progressed to explaining why the toilet was not a carwash for Matchbox cars and pleading with kids to put away their toys, lest we have another Lego incident involving Dad's foot and a few choice words. Needless to say, I yearned to talk to adults—to have real conversations!

When I heard the words "free child care," I truly didn't care what book we were going to study—I was in!

THE POWER OF A RADICAL RELATIONSHIP

"God gives us what we need wrapped in what we want." How deeply I would learn the truth of this saying by Jeff Cavins during the course of that Bible study! Little did I know that my casual encounter with Nichole at the back-to-school night would radically change the trajectory of my life.

A few days before the Bible study began, I went to a local Catholic bookstore and bought the Revised Standard Version—Catholic Edition, the one recommended on the Great Adventure website. After stopping at Office Max to buy a sassy three-ringed binder, one with pockets and a protective zipped cover, I also bought the best pens I could afford and even picked up a highlighter that was specifically made to not bleed through pages. One night, after the kids fell asleep, I carefully applied the Bible Timeline Bible tabs to each of the seventy-three books of the Bible.

I'm so ready! I thought to myself.

On the first day of our Bible study, we gathered at a little church by my house, forty women and about a kajillion children. After checking our kids into the free childcare, we grabbed something to eat and began listening to a video featuring Jeff Cavins, the creator and founder of the study. (Yes, this was before the invention of DVDs, but post the invention of the wheel.)

After the engaging and humorous introduction, I looked around the room and saw some of the busiest women in the world relaxed and smiling. How could this be? How could these women, who

6

were so busy they could rarely find the time to shave *both* legs, be enthralled by someone asking them to read and study the Bible?

"When you decide to read the Bible, the first thing you do is, you go out and buy a new Bible.... Why? Because the old one won't work," Jeff proclaimed from the video. The room instantly filled with chuckles.

"And you get the best pen money can buy, because you need to write down your very important insights" he added.

Wow, does this guy know me, or what? I thought. —Ha.

Of course he didn't know me from Adam (or Eve), but he did know the Bible, and he knew how to build a strong relationship with the Lord. He also knew how to relate to his students, whether they were sitting in front of him or thousands of miles away watching him on a television screen.

Over the next few weeks, I began my daily routine of "Scripture study." When my kids were taking their naps or watching *Dora the Explorer*, I sat at the kitchen table with my Bible open before me. I dove into the book of Genesis and began learning about salvation history. My mind was filled with new insights, perspectives, and questions. My faith was growing. I loved all that I was learning.

After a few weeks of studying the Bible, I ran into Jeff Cavins at a grade school Christmas pageant. I'll never forget it. First, because I literally ran into him as we were jockeying for the best position to get pictures of our kids, and second, because that encounter helped me to see that God was beckoning me to use my gifts.

After clicking my camera, I looked up and recognized the familiar face.

"Jeff Cavins, my name is Kelly Wahlquist. I'm taking your Bible study, and I love it!"

"That's wonderful," he said. As I kept an eye on stage, watching for my little angel to appear, I continued to talk to Jeff.

"There's only one thing about the study that I don't like," I said, my voice blending in with the chatter of other proud parents.

"What's that?"

"That I didn't invent it! It's how my brain works!" I replied, laughing.

As the school band began playing, we walked backed to our seats, still laughing and chatting.

"Your friend Nichole told me you have some leadership qualities. You should consider leading a Bible study someday!" Jeff continued.

After the last verse of "Silent Night" was sung and the curtain dropped on yet another successful Christmas story told by children, I kept thinking, *There is no way that I could ever lead a Bible study! I'm just barely out of the book of Genesis. I've got seventy-two books left to learn!*

But a month later, I began leading our Bible study. Now, almost a decade later, I am still working with Jeff to spread the Gospel. How did this all happen? Well, I think it happened because others saw gifts in me that I didn't even know I had. And God drew me into relationships that could help me cultivate those gifts, as he does with each of us.

Before I signed up for that Bible study, my life was, in a sense, what I had dreamed of since I was a little girl. I was married to a wonderful man, had three beautiful children, and a job I loved working as a nursing supervisor. I was close to my family and had wonderful friends. Yet, I was longing for something more. As St. Augustine once said, my heart was "restless" and I was yearning to rest in God. What I needed, without even knowing it, was a deep and personal relationship with God. And luckily for me, God was reeling me in, using my sneaky, dear friend Nichole and a gifted Bible teacher to help him do it.

The *Catechism of the Catholic Church* tells us, "The desire for God is written in the human heart, because man is created by God and for God; and God never ceases to draw man to himself" (CCC 27). When I think about this quote, I delight that Nichole had the "guts" to put my name on that list—an action that to this day she contends she can't believe she did. It was because it was all part of God's plan of sheer goodness. God thirsts for us that we might thirst for him.

What a radical concept! The Lord of the universe thirsts for us. He wants to be our friend, our personal companion on this journey we call life. But here's an equally radical thought: The bonds we share with family, friends, colleagues, and even the strangers we meet each day have eternal significance. Often, it's these ordinary relationships that draw us into a life-changing relationship with Christ. Every connection we make with our brothers and sisters on earth holds great power. Each day, God calls us to be in community, to share faith and friendship, and to lead each other into a beautiful, miraculous, and radical relationship with God.

Are you feeling restless? Do you thirst for God? Do you long to develop a deeper more meaningful relationship with Christ? Try looking into the faces of the people you meet each day. They are God's instruments, holy messengers of God's truth and compassion. They will teach you what it means to be a follower of Christ.

9

Through them you will come to understand the beautiful relationship of the Father, Son, and Holy Spirit. They will help you gain new perspectives into the power of prayer and the sacraments. As you build relationships with the faithful (and not so faithful) you will learn how to say to yes to God, as our Blessed Mother did. While building bonds with the saints, you will receive sacred gifts of friendship and know true communion with heaven.

We have been created for relationship. God weaves our lives together in a beautiful tapestry that reflects his love and compassion to the world. In the coming chapters, we'll discover how radical these relationships can be.

TOOLS FOR BUILDING YOUR RELATIONSHIPS
Scripture

Read the story of Jesus meeting the Samaritan woman at the well in John 4:7–10 and then read it a second time more slowly. Then read it for a third time, noting the words or insights that jump out at you. Write down those words and the thoughts you had about them.

Meditation

Imagine yourself visiting the Holy Land. You are hiking in Samaria and you come across Jacob's well. Because you are thirsty, you approach the well to pull up some water. Just as you arrive at the well, Jesus walks up to you. You recognize him, and you are amazed. You say, "Oh my! Hello, Lord. I just stopped here to quench my thirst. I have hiked a long way." He says, "Go ahead and get some water." You drop the rope with a bucket on it into the well and pull up some water to drink. He smiles at you as you gulp the water. You look at him. He keeps smiling at you and seems to be looking right into your soul. Then he says, "Are you satisfied? I mean *really* satisfied? Do you not want the living water that I give that quenches the deepest thirst in your soul?" What is your reply?

QUESTIONS FOR REFLECTION AND DISCUSSION

1. What people in your life were "surprise relationships," ones you didn't expect to become close friendships? How did they lead you closer to God? How did the Lord bring these encounters into your life? What did you learn about yourself or about God?

2. What about your life was what the world would call "perfect" before you recognized that you longed for something more? Did you ever think of God's longing for you? How does that thought change your relationship with God right now?

3. What special gift has God given you in the past that was wrapped up in what you wanted? What do you want now from God? What might be wrapped up inside of that current want? Are you aware of any needs—physical, familial, relational, or spiritual—for yourself?

4. Mother Teresa helps us realize the *thirst* of Jesus on the cross for each one of us. Is God's thirst for you to be with him a new thought for you? Do you desire to be in close relationship with God? In other words, do you want to be a saint and respond to God's desire for you?

5. Which person in your life today could be waiting for you to bring God's message of desire to them? What opportunities are there for speaking to that person, writing him or her a note, or just praying silently that God might use you to set that person's heart on fire for a deeper relationship with him?

LIVING YOUR RELATIONAL GIFT

Option 1: Among the adult friends you know, choose to have lunch with one. During your lunch conversation, tell that friend about your prayers for her (or him). At the end of your time together, ask that person to pray for you—specifically for something that has your relationship with others or your relationship with God at its center.

Option 2: Write a list of God's personal gifts to you, some which have come from out of nowhere, others through people you've met or even know well. Think about how those gifts have changed you or the direction of your life. Write a thank you note to God for one (not more than two) of them, indicating what it is that has changed for which you are very grateful.

soul work — not body work, but healthy body as vessel for soul

CHAPTER TWO

Who's Your "They"?

Early one September morning—and I do mean early—I arrived at the Baton Rouge airport en route home to Minnesota via a connecting flight in Atlanta. As I mentioned in the previous chapter, my life had taken a turn. Two years after Nichole had signed me up for that Bible study, I left my job in the medical field where I was aspiring to be director of nursing. Now I was the director of Community Relations for *The Great Adventure Catholic Bible Study,* coordinating Bible studies around the United States and Canada, organizing pilgrimages to the Holy Land, and running the National Catholic Bible Conference.

I had loved working in the medical field, especially caring for the sick and elderly. But I was happy in my new position, and it felt like the two jobs were very much connected. As a nurse, I worked to heal the body; now my job was to heal the soul. I was traveling the country and teaching leaders (busy men and women like myself) how to implement, run, and grow fruitful Bible studies. More importantly, I was sharing my conversion story and helping others develop a personal relationship with the Lord.

That Sunday morning, I was coming back from giving a Bible study leadership seminar. It was so early that not even a single coffee shop was open, and that made me just a *wee bit* crabby. On the short flight to Atlanta, I couldn't stop thinking about a large nonfat vanilla latte. When we finally landed in the Peach State, praise God—all the coffee shops were open! I looked at my watch. *Shoot!* There was no time to stop for a cup of morning brew. I had to run at lightning speed to catch my next flight. High heels in hand, computer bag over my shoulder, and carry-on suitcase rolling wildly behind me, I got crabbier as I passed each barista. "I need coffee..." I whined to myself.

When I finally reached my gate, I was even more irritated. The place was beyond crowded! Three planes were scheduled to depart within thirty minutes of each other. There was no place to sit and barely room to stand. Four hundred travelers were packed into one area like sardines, but they didn't seem to care. Almost every person had assumed the "iTravel" stance—head down, eyes fixed on their smartphone, iPad or laptop, fingers frantically typing to get out what was, no doubt, a very important message. Everyone was consumed with his or her own business, and I was right there too. Suddenly, the sea of self-absorption was shaken by a bloodcurdling scream. With one collective glance, the crowd turned toward the place where the scream seemed to have had originated.

Now, in the Atlanta airport, they had (and may still have) self-compacting garbage cans. If you haven't seen these, take my word: They are scary! Moments after you put your garbage into them, you hear this fierce sound, like a monster growling, and then in an instant your garbage is squashed to a tenth of the size of what it once was. They even have warning signs on them telling people to stand clear of them (for fear of losing life and limb perhaps!).

In the place where the scream had come from was a young mother wearing worn-out jeans and her hair in a ponytail. With a backpack slung over her shoulder, her shirt stained with spit-up, and her toddler fidgeting in a stroller, she was comforting a woman who was so upset she could barely speak. "Ma'am, can I help you?" the mother asked the panicked stranger.

Every traveler was now watching the two women, as though we were the audience at a theater. Everyone was quiet, waiting to see what would happen next.

"This garbage can just ate my ticket, and my flight is boarding in five minutes!" said the panicked woman.

Calmly, the young mom put down her backpack and rolled up her sleeve. Bravely she reached into the flesh-eating garbage can. Within seconds, her arm emerged, and in the gentlest of voices she asked her new acquaintance:

"Is this your boarding pass?"

Just a few moments earlier, the terrifying shriek of one woman had brought hundreds of preoccupied travelers to a standstill. Now, that same woman was tranquil, clutching her plane ticket like it was a priceless treasure.

"Thank you!" said the woman, her gratitude evidenced by the serene look on her face.

"Don't mention it," said the mom.

One man began clapping, and in seconds four hundred travelers followed suite, the place erupting in applause.

This is incredible, I thought.

Another man stood up and pointed to the young mother. "You, you're the one! You're the one who does something nice for one person, and they turn around and do something nice for someone else. You're the one who changes the world!"

I sat there, completely floored. I had gone from being irritable and consumed with myself to watching a radical exchange of love

15

and compassion. I knew I had just witnessed the body of Christ in action. For me, it was a moment of spiritual transformation.

CREATED FOR RELATIONSHIP

As I got on the plane, I couldn't stop thinking about the bond that was forged between those two women in the airport. The experience reminded me that women—in a special way—are created for relationships: wonderful, amazing, radical relationships.

I thought of a story from the Gospel of Luke. Jesus was teaching a large crowd that had gathered. The Pharisees and teachers of the law were sitting close by. The disciples were there, too. Then, a group of men tried to make their way through the crowd. They were carrying their friend, a paralyzed man on a stretcher. The Scripture tell us that, "They sought to bring him in and lay him before Jesus" (Luke 5:18).

Think about that. The friends "sought" to bring their friend into the presence of Christ. Their friendship must have been strong, because when they saw they couldn't reach Jesus, they carried the man's bed up to the roof, removed the tiles, and lowered him down before Jesus. That's some plan B! These men, moved by love, creatively accomplished an important mission. They brought their buddy to God. Jesus saw *their* faith and healed the man. If any relationship is radical, it's one that leads to the healing of another through an encounter with Christ.

I once heard Jeff Cavins teach about this story while in the Holy Land. As he read from the Gospel of Luke, he highlighted the word *they*.

"*They* were bringing a man in on his bed..."

"*They* sought to bring him in and lay him before Jesus..."

"*They* went up on the roof and let him down with his bed through the tiles…"

When Jesus saw their faith he healed the man. And then Jeff asked, "Who are your *they*? Who has brought *you* to Christ?"

As I was flying back to Minnesota, I thought of times in my life when I had been paralyzed and friends had carried me to Jesus.

There was a time when my life changed in an instant and I feared I would lose all that was near and dear to me—above all, I feared I would lose dozens of relationships. After five years traveling the country to promote the *Great Bible Adventure Bible Study*, my position with the company was moved to the East Coast. There was no way I could uproot my family and move across the country, no matter how much I loved my job.

My heart sank and my stomach literally ached as I envisioned friendships, embedded deep in my heart, coming to a drastic halt. I couldn't understand why this was happening. My nicely ordered life seemed to be turning upside down. I didn't know what God's plan was. How could I know that within a few weeks, another job would open up for me, an exciting position working in the greater ministry of evangelization?

What I feared never happened. Instead, the friends I thought I would lose reached out to me in my time of need. My phone rang off the hook. They were calling to encourage, support, and help me go forward. They lifted me up in prayer. For months, not a day went by that I didn't get a text message, a phone call, or an e-mail that said, "Praying for you today." They made sure I kept my focus on Jesus by sending me articles, books, notes, and Scripture passages to inspire me.

In a sense, *they* were removing the "tiles" that were beginning to separate me from the Lord—*they* were knocking down the barriers of doubt, fear, and despair. In my time of trial, I believe *they* each played a part in helping me develop a new and intimate relationship with the three most important Persons in my life— God the Father, God the Son, and God the Holy Spirit.

As my plane landed in the Land of 10,000 Lakes, I found myself thanking God for all the women who had carried me to the Lord. Their love and compassion had prepared me to be a spokesperson for Christ.

A few months later, I realized just how powerful this preparation had been. I was being interviewed on a Catholic podcast, and I shared the impact Jeff's teaching had on me and how it caused me to ponder all the relationships I have had along the way that have drawn me closer to the Lord.

"The Lord has brought many new relationships into my life, relationships that have led me to him. So many people over the past few years have been my 'they,' and someday if I meet them in heaven, I'm going to do what Jeff said. I'm going to ask them to stand up so I can thank them," I told the radio audience.

The interviewer, Deacon Tom Fox, put a spin on it that stopped me in my tracks. He said, "Kelly, you travel the country telling people about the Lord. Think about all those people who are now or will be in heaven who will stand up and thank *you* for being one of their 'they.'" The concept blew me away. For some crazy reason, though I was out encouraging people to read Scripture and to learn and love their faith, I suddenly understood my calling in whole new way. Like the friends in the Gospel story, my mission was to carry people to Christ.

This radical mission is not reserved for me, or Jeff Cavins, or those who are great leaders in our Church. God invites each of us be a "they"

to be a "they" in our everyday lives. Perhaps as you look back on your life, you'll discover that God has placed relationships in your life for a reason. Think about times when you have faced a crisis. Have there been friends who have brought you into the presence of Christ through prayer, supportive calls, text messages, meals, or maybe even the simple gift of presence? Have you known the comfort of being lifted from your pain by a sister or brother in Christ? Perhaps a special friend has helped you retrieve goodness from the garbage can of your struggles.

It's an honor to share the love of Christ, isn't it? As we befriend those who are paralyzed by fear, illness, failure, or loss, we are loving them as Christ would. We are sharing in the Gospel story of the faithful friends who lowered their buddy to Jesus. We are building holy and beautiful relationships with the people God has entrusted to our care. Our mission, if we choose to accept it, is to carry our friends to Jesus.

Tools for Building Your Relationships

Scripture

Read the story of Jesus healing the paralytic in Luke 5:17–26, then read it a second time more slowly. Then read it for a third time, noting the words or insights that jump out at you. Write down those words and the thoughts you had about them.

Meditation

Think of a friend who has helped you when you were in a tough spot, someone who came to your rescue in a time of difficulty. Write down what happened and how that friend came to your aid. What did he or she do? Ask the Lord, "Lord, were you in this?" Listen to his answer. Then, give thanks to the Lord for that friend.

Remember a time when you helped a friend in need.

QUESTIONS FOR REFLECTION AND DISCUSSION

1. In Luke 5:17–26, we learn that friends took a paralytic to Jesus to be healed. The Pharisees witnessed this relationship—compassion toward a friend—yet questioned Jesus's power to heal. What can we learn about the power of relationships in growing closer to Christ?

2. Many saints provide us with great examples of living in close spiritual relationship with God. Who is your favorite saint? How did that saint grow in friendship with our Lord? How did this saint stay close to God?

3. In his homily on the Feast of Saints Peter and Paul, June 29, 2011, Pope Benedict defined friendship with our Lord as the "communion of the will." How does the world define friendship? What are some superficial aspects of friendship that steer us away from Jesus?

4. Looking back, can you identify relationships that were instrumental (perhaps life-changing) in helping you form a closer relationship with Christ?

5. Who are the friends, coworkers, or even acquaintances present in your life? Examining these relationships, how might God be calling you to bring those people closer to his Son?

LIVING YOUR RELATIONAL GIFT

Option 1: Decide to applaud someone today. Look for someone you don't know who is doing something that is kind, generous, or even just patient. Point out their goodness to them. Thank them for their kindness. Perhaps say, "Thank you for making our day more loving."

Option 2: The person you know as a "paralytic" in your life needs your prayers. Set aside a specific time to pray for them or select a daily Mass to attend, which you can offer specifically for the spiritual needs of this person. Send them a card with the notation that you prayed specifically for them, or telling them you offered your Mass for them.

CHAPTER THREE

God Is So Big

I always thought I would be the mom of four boys. When I was six months pregnant with our first child, my husband asked: "If it's a girl, can we name her Annika?" Knowing, of course, that there was no way I was having a daughter, I said, "Sure, name her Petunia, if you want." After eight hours of labor, the doctor placed a little girl in my arms. And you know what? An extraordinary bond was created when I first glanced at the newborn face of my baby. Though I wasn't prepared for a daughter, I loved her immediately.

Shortly after Annika was born, my mother said: "Just wait and see. You will love all of your children the same, but you will have a different relationship with each one." Turns out, my mom was right. I love all three of my children equally, but my relationship with each is tremendously different.

My oldest daughter has no fear. At the age of four, she learned how to waterski, and in her senior year of high school, she sang in front of 25,000 people. Though I definitely wouldn't sing in front of 25,000 (for many reasons), Annika and I spend hours laughing at the same things, have deep conversations about faith and life, and enjoy any kind of grammatical quip—like the "sexy dash."

My middle daughter, Alannah, could shop for hours, yet she has trouble being separated from her friends for minutes, something I can totally relate to. She's a bit more serious, but the two of us rarely drive anywhere without cranking up the country music. After two girls came my little guy, with a heart of gold. Not a night goes by that he doesn't want to snuggle. (Somebody, please tell me when he shoots up to six foot five, he'll still feel this way.) Though I love all three of them equally, I have a different relationship with each one. Each of them has unique and wonderful gifts that make them who they are.

Perhaps our family is a bit like yours. Though we all have a variety of interests and personalities, we share a bond of love that can never be broken. Though we are unique in our own ways, as a family we are unified.

The Trinity, though a difficult concept to understand, can be understood in the context of a loving family. Though we relate to the Father, Son, and Spirit in different ways, we share a perfect communion with each one. Hmmm...perfect communion—how does that work? How do we grow in relationship with a three-in-one God? What an intense question! Let's try to answer it by looking at each person of the Trinity.

GOD IS SO BIG

When I was in preschool, my image of God was the Statue of Liberty. I know that sounds crazy, but as a little four-year-old, I knew God was big, and the Statue of Liberty was the biggest thing I had ever seen. When I looked at the statue, I saw God carrying a book and lifting high a torch. I remember thinking: *God is big, but he is so far away. He's all by himself on an island.* That image of an aloof God stayed with me for many years.

Once I had children of my own, I had a new perspective on the role of God the Father. As I looked through the lens of a parent, it was easier to see God, not as some enormous far-off, ungraspable being, but rather as a loving Father, a dad who is always present and looking out for his children.

If you are a parent (or if you have ever babysat a toddler!), I'm sure you can relate to this scenario. One night while I was making dinner, I noticed an eerie quietness in the room. Rounding the corner, I instantly saw why. Myles, my two-year-old son, had stopped making his usual truck sounds. Instead, he was jumping joyfully on the sofa. In an instant, my eyes took in the corner of the coffee table and the antique lamp from my Great-Grandma Sally. I also saw the two-and-a-half foot drop from the couch to the wood floor. Without hesitation, I caught Myles in mid-jump and firmly said: "No jumping on the couch!"

I wasn't trying to ruin his fun, threaten his freedom, or show my power over this little two-footer. Of course not! As a loving parent, I was aware of the dangers that accompany couch jumping. It was my responsibility to keep him safe, and I was acting out of love.

Just as I can now foresee the physical dangers that surround my children, God, our Heavenly Father, knows the dangers that surround our souls. He doesn't want anything to impede the ultimate goal of our spiritual life: union with him. God knows our every weakness and our need for continuous, loving guidance to avoid the dangers that threaten our chances of spending eternity with him in heaven. I can't even tell you the number of times my Heavenly Father has scooped me into the safety of his embrace when I was, no doubt, bouncing off into danger without even knowing it.

I now realize that my four-year-old image of God wasn't too far off the mark. God *is* big. Like the Statue of Liberty, he is awesome to behold, but fortunately for us, he is never aloof or absent from our lives. He's a protective and loving father, with us always. In fact, at every moment and in every situation, he's reaching out to us to bring us home to his heart. He has given us the greatest book ever, the Bible, to guide us back to a relationship with him, and he has given us a torch, the Light of the World, his only begotten Son, to light the way.

A Personal Relationship with Jesus

When I was growing up, I loved the Blessed Virgin Mary. I loved singing songs about her with my Auntie Mary Jane as we traveled the streets of St. Paul in her station wagon. As a little girl, my grandmother let me play with her rosary, and I loved brushing my small fingers over the beads. At Christmastime, after my mother read me stories about Mary, I'd often place a small, carved figure of the Blessed Mother in our manger scene.

In fact, one of my greatest childhood memories happened at my First Holy Communion which took place at the celebration Mass of my grandparents' fiftieth wedding anniversary. After Communion the musicians played "On This Day, O Beautiful Mother." As I stood at the altar, in a white dress and veil, I placed a rose in the vase before a statue of Mary, my beautiful Mother. My Auntie Lani sat in a nearby pew, smiling. As a music liturgist, she had planned the whole thing. I remember standing there, looking at Mary smiling down at me, and having a feeling of complete contentment as I waited for the song to end. (Now, as a seven-year-old, that's probably not how I would have explained it, but I felt really happy.)

My relationship with Mary has always been deep and personal. Maybe this is because so many women in my life have encouraged me to seek her guidance. My mother, grandmother, and aunts taught me that Mary holds a special place in God's heart. So too, I've found a special place in my heart for her.

But though I've always talked to Mary and asked her to pray for me, I didn't have a deep and personal relationship with her Son. Don't get me wrong, I knew all about Jesus. My favorite part of grade school was sitting at the feet of the Franciscan sisters as they read to us about Jesus. I especially remember Sr. Vera reading from the Gospel of Matthew: "Let the children come to me, and do not hinder them; for to such belongs the kingdom of heaven" (Matthew 19:14). As I imagined myself leaning on Jesus, all I could think was: *I never want to grow up; I want Jesus to always think I am special.*

Throughout the whole story of salvation, from Adam and Eve to the Apostles, we learn over and over that God is always faithful to his word and to his people. Through Jesus, God shares his faithfulness with us in a gift of friendship. It's a radical friendship that leads us to his heart—and ultimately to his cross and resurrection.

Over the years, people have asked if I have a personal relationship with the Lord. It's a question that brings to mind many conversion stories that I have heard. One woman once told me that she saw the face of Jesus comforting her during childbirth. Another man remembered the night he pulled his car to the side of the road and tearfully gave his life to the Lord. Then there was the lady who felt the presence of Christ so strongly that she changed her wayward life in an instant.

I once assumed that a personal encounter with Jesus had to be some big "St. Paul" conversion. (If you don't know this story, it's a good one about Saul literally being knocked over by the love of

Jesus. You can read it in Acts 9:1–31. Go check it out; it's a quick read.) But the Lord showed me that I didn't need a lightning-bolt conversion experience. I simply needed to grow closer to the Jesus I was introduced to as a child; the Jesus who says: "Let the little children come to me, for such is the kingdom of heaven."

As I look back on my spiritual journey, my encounters with Jesus have been simple but extremely profound. Sometimes, when I read my Bible, especially the Gospels, I feel so much joy that I simply can't put it down. When I sit before the Blessed Sacrament, I am often encompassed by the presence of Christ, so much so that I am overwhelmed with an unexplainable peace. At Mass, when the priest lifts the consecrated host, and I remember the death of Jesus, an indescribable gratitude fills me. One Sunday when I received the Eucharist, the truth of redemptive suffering was revealed to me. "Your suffering matters," I heard Jesus say in my heart. These sacred moments have radically strengthened my faith and drawn me into a deep relationship with my Savior.

My relationship with Jesus continues to grow each day. I talk to him in the car, chat with him while doing the dishes, laugh with him when I think of some theological pun, and look forward to waking up early to just sit and listen to him in the stillness of the morning. He is my best friend, the big brother I look to for everything. For me, this friendship didn't begin with a big dramatic bang; instead it was the result of a persistent invitation from the Lord to enter into a relationship with him, a prayer to know him better answered, and of course, a lifelong relationship with his Mother.

The Lent before Nichole signed me up for the Bible study, I prayed I would get to know Jesus a little better. What I got that following fall, and continue to receive, is a relationship with Jesus that has broadened my understanding of a God who longs to befriend us. Think about it: Jesus, the faithful God of our salvation, wants to be in union with us—and he doesn't need some drastic means by which to do that. He just wants to be our friend. And what do you do with friends? You give them one-on-one time, you look at them with love, you listen to them with an open heart, you tell them what they mean to you, you trust them, you depend on them, you share everything with them, and you accept them for who they are. What a glorious invitation we have been given!

These days, when I remember my First Communion, I know why I felt such contentment. That day, I believe that Mary was looking down on me and saying, "Kelly needs to know my Son."

Mary was like the men who carried their buddy to Jesus in the Gospel of Luke. She brought me to the Savior of the world. As our heavenly mother, she carries all of God's children into a deep and personal relationship with her Son. And a friendship with Jesus is the most radical gift we can ever receive.

COME, HOLY SPIRIT!

I didn't grow up with the Holy Spirit. I know that sounds crazy, because of course I was baptized and confirmed in the Catholic Church. I knew the Holy Spirit dwelled within me and was at work in my life, but he wasn't someone I talked about much, and certainly was not someone I talked to—no way! Growing up, he was referred to as the "Holy Ghost," and there was no way I wanted anything to do with a ghost, unless that ghost had his own Saturday morning cartoon show, was friendly, and answered to the name of Casper.

But a few years ago, I had an experience that caused me to look at the Holy Spirit in a whole new way. My friend Lauretta, who lived in a suburb of Chicago, invited me to a Filipino charismatic conference. To be honest, I didn't know what to expect. When I walked into the gathering, I was taken aback by hundreds of people raising their hands, speaking in tongues, and praising the Lord with emphatic voices.

It was intriguing to see people praying with such passion and conviction. But what really caught my attention was the hospitality and the intense sense of approval I felt from the Filipino women. They surrounded me with kindness so naturally and received me so warmly into their community. Though I didn't quite understand the expressive outpouring of the Holy Spirit, it didn't seem to matter to them—I was their sister in Christ.

Not only did these charismatic women have an awesome relationship with God, but their care for one another was like nothing I'd ever seen. They were in true communion with one another. They prayed and sang together. They seemed to know each other's stories. They were filled with irrepressible joy. I wanted what they had. I didn't even really know what it was, but I wanted it. I wanted the Holy Spirit to be alive and active in my life like he was in theirs. And on that day, for the first time, I began to communicate with the Third Person of the Trinity.

Have you ever experienced the power of the Holy Spirit working in your life? Perhaps you've heard the voice of the Spirit leading you to help a stranger or to forgive someone who has hurt you. Maybe you've been prompted to pray for a friend or take a certain job. Maybe you've just had a great peace about a huge, life-changing decision.

St. John Paul II said, "Whenever the Spirit intervenes, he leaves people astonished. He brings about events of amazing newness; he radically changes persons and history."[5] I have to tell you, St. John Paul the Great was right! Since I've allowed myself to be open to the work of the Holy Spirit, my life has been full of astonishing events that have radically changed my history.

A few years ago, I had an incredible experience with the Holy Spirit when I attended a Called to Lead conference, an event geared to help leaders share the Word of God. At the time, I barely knew how to find my way through the Bible, much less lead anyone else through it.

As I walked into the conference, I looked around and saw hundreds of people. They all had Bibles, Bible bags, special Bible markers, pens, and notebooks, Catholic commentaries, and books on how to study the Bible. I took a deep breath and thought, *I am so far out of my league.*

While I sat by myself, waiting for the conference to begin, I said to myself: "These people are so much holier than I am..."

After fidgeting for a while, I decided I really didn't belong and got up to leave. But something in my heart prompted me to stay, so I settled back into my spot among the masses.

I kept asking the Lord: "What am I doing here?"

Even though thoughts of doubt kept surfacing, an inner voice said, "Stay, Kelly...there's something here for you."

So I surrendered. "OK, Lord, I don't know why you brought me here, but you must have some plan. I'll be open to listening tonight...but I'm not promising I'll return tomorrow."

Just then, one of the speakers took the stage and began to speak.

"If you are here tonight, it's not because you got in your car and you drove all the way out to Chanhassen, Minnesota, and you walked into St. Hubert's and you sat down in your seat. If you're sitting here tonight, it's because God has a plan for your life, and he wants to tell you about it."

Wow! I couldn't believe it. It was like God was talking directly to me. The conversation I had heard in my heart was a conversation with the Spirit of God, and he heard me in no uncertain terms. He even used the exact words. He made sure I knew he was talking to me.

This is what I call a Holy Spirit two-by-four. Sometimes I feel as though the Holy Spirit has to knock me over the head with a heavenly plank of wood to get my attention. Well, that night, he got my attention. I stayed for the entire conference. What I learned is that it's good to pay attention to the voice of the Spirit. Two years later, I spoke at the very conference I didn't think I belonged at. The Holy Spirit must have a good sense of humor, too!

In his book *In His Spirit: A Guide to Today's Spirituality*, Fr. Richard Hauser, S.J., writes about the importance of being in tune with third person of the Trinity: "It should always be remembered that the Spirit we receive is the same Spirit that moved Jesus. As we open ourselves more and more to the influence of this spirit, we come closer to Jesus and ever more like him."[6]

Ever since that day back at the Filipino charismatic conference, I have asked the Holy Spirit to guide me, and he has done that tenfold. As a result, my relationship with him is on fire. Not a morning goes by that I don't say, "Come, Holy Spirit" before my feet hit the floor. Tomorrow morning, why not invite the Holy Spirit to fill your day with the power of his presence? As you are feeding the kids breakfast or driving to work, just pray: "Come, Holy Spirit." You might find that your busy, everyday life will be marked with sacred promptings and the quiet whispers of our Savior.

RELATING TO A BIG GOD

As we grow and change, so too do our relationships. Just as my relationship with my earthly father has changed as I've gone from crawling to walking to skipping off to kindergarten to walking down the aisle on my wedding day, my relationship with my heavenly Father, his Son, and the Holy Spirit also have changed. Like so many of my sisters in Christ, I've grown in ways I could never have imagined years ago. In the past ten years, my relationship with Jesus has undergone the most radical change of all, and I am now teaching others about him.

But we are *all* called to do the will of the Father and proclaim the Son with the help of the Holy Spirit. When we enter into relationship with each person of the Trinity, we are strengthened for this important mission. In communion with the Trinity, we can live out God's purpose for our lives with certitude and joy.

God is so big—he's a three-in-one God, a Trinity of loving relationship, a family. God gives himself to us as Father, Son, and Spirit. And this big God longs to be in relationship with *us*. As a loving parent, he protects us and shields us from harm. Through Jesus, our Savior, he calls us his friends. His Holy Spirit moves in us, with us, through us. And here's the best part: We were created to relate to our Triune God and to share his love and grace with the world.

TOOLS FOR BUILDING YOUR RELATIONSHIPS
Scripture

Read the verse from St. Paul's greeting to the Philippians in Philippians 1:2, and then read it a second time more slowly. Then read it for a third time noting the words or insights that jump out at you. Write down those words and the thoughts you had about them.

Meditation

Sit quietly in prayer. In your imagination picture the Blessed Mother coming to you, taking your hand, and saying, "I have come to introduce you to the Blessed Trinity." She leads you into heaven and into a radiant room. There, three majestic persons are seated on a golden bench watching you approach. Mary says, "Meet our Heavenly Father; meet Jesus, my Son; meet the Holy Spirit, my spouse." As you gaze in wonderment at the threesome, one seems to reach out to you saying, "I want us to get better acquainted!"

Which one seems to be reaching out to you? What is your response?

QUESTIONS FOR REFLECTION AND DISCUSSION

1. In John 3:16–18, we learn that God is love. Thus, it follows that there must be a "lover, beloved, and love" in the Holy Trinity. Many theologians say that God is the supreme relationship. How do you experience the love of God through each person of the Trinity—the Father, the Son, and the Holy Spirit?

2. Many theologians suggest that the Trinitarian relationship is ultimately about being for the other—existing for another. The doctrine of the Trinity is about being with and for each other. In which of your relationships are you with and for the other? How are your decisions about this person with and for him or her?

3. Is there a scriptural passage or a saint's devotion that helps you understand this Trinitarian relationship?

4. Recollect and review your relationship with Mary the Mother of Jesus. How has she mothered you? How do you speak or pray to her? Are there any special requests you have placed in her hands? Has she gently led you to Jesus? Have you asked her to do so?

5. Trinitarian love is about total self-giving. Is there a relationship in your life that needs reconciling? How can the Father, the Son, or the Holy Spirit help you in this relationship? By the same token, is there a relationship in your life that is especially beautiful? How are the characteristics of Trinitarian love manifested?

LIVING YOUR RELATIONAL GIFT

Option 1: Review your family relationships—both the family you were born into and the family in which you live now. How is each individual relationship different? Focus on the relationship that is the most distant. What might you do to enliven that relationship or make it closer? Make a plan to concentrate your efforts at enhancing that family relationship and carry it out.

Option 2: Each Person of the Trinity reflects deference, love, and blessing to each other—a true giving and receiving the gift of self. Imagine that they are inviting you to join them. What do you bring to this gathering? What gifts do you have to offer? What is it that you desire from the Persons of the Holy Trinity? Write down your gifts and what you desire from their inclusive love of you. Bring that scrap of paper to Church the next time you attend Mass. Read it as an offering and as a request for giving and receiving love.

CHAPTER FOUR

Woman—Created to Relate

Every Christmas Peter comes home from college and wisely uses the wafting smell of freshly brewed Folgers coffee to awaken his parents and alert them of his return. Every time I see this commercial, I cry. Now granted, as the mother of a child in college, some of my tears are out of pity for his parents who probably have been footing the bill for his college tuition since 1985.

But the truth is, my tears stem from the fact that Folgers hits a nerve. They have tapped into my emotions and connected me to the relationships in Peter's family. My husband never cries at this commercial, though he has been known to mutter something under his breath about how his kids better graduate before the next millennium. So why is it that this scenario always tugs at my heartstrings and those of women all around the country? The answer is simple. Women are uniquely oriented to relationship.

FROM THE BEGINNING

So where did woman get their relational capabilities? Or, to phrase the question differently: Why do we cry when we watch commercials about coffee? Theologian Dr. Deborah Savage does an excellent job addressing this question by taking us back to the beginning and examining the two creation accounts.[7]

In the first account of creation, found in Genesis 1, we see God creating in a particular order, almost as if he is checking things off in the ultimate day planner: Light and darkness, day one...check; Heaven above, water below, day two...check; Dry land, grass, flowers, trees...check, check, check, check, day three complete. The next two days, God creates the sun, moon and stars, and on day four it's the fish, followed by the birds on day five. The cattle, the beasts of the earth and the creeping things come to life on day six. "It is good..." God says. And then God said, "Let us make man in our image, after our likeness..." and he created "man in his own image, in the image of God he created him; male and female he created them." Again, God said: "It is good." Finally, on the seventh day, God put down his day planner and rested.

In the second account of creation, in Genesis 2, we see God creating Adam from dust and breathing life into him. God creates a beautiful garden, "pleasant to the sight and good for food" (Genesis 2:9), and he puts Adam in charge of caring for the garden. Not a bad first job; not a bad first boss. The Lord knows it is not good for man to be alone, so he gives Adam some animals to keep him company, and as we all know, whenever company arrives, the work load increases. Adam now has to name each one of animals—a task no doubt made much easier by the fact that Adam did not own a copy of *25,001 Best Baby Names* and had no one to argue with his choice of a name. Although personally named by Adam, none of the animals prove to be a fit helper for him, so while Adam slept; God took a rib from his side and created Eve. Then God brought Eve to Adam.

It is Dr. Savage's exploration into this second account of creation that really struck me, because she offers some really cool insights into the relational nature of women.

In Genesis 2:15, Adam is created from dust and awakens as God breathes life into his soul. Aside from God, Adam's first encounter with reality is the Garden of Eden—the garden which he is to "till and keep." In Hebrew the words are *abad* and *shamar*—*abad* meaning to work or serve, and *shamar* meaning to exercise great care over. So Adam's first orientation is one of work and things. His first glimpse of reality is an understanding of work.

Eve, aside from her encounter with God, is first oriented toward Adam. Her first contact with reality is Adam, a person. Eve is created for relationship. She is created to be Adam's helper, but not just any old helper. The Hebrew word in Scripture for helper is *ezer*, and it does not mean "servant" or "slave." It means divine helper, an equal partner! Eve has been built out of Adam's very side and designed for a relationship with him.

From the very beginning we see the beauty of man and woman, both created in the image and likeness of God.[8] Their relationship was meant to be complementary, a coming together of two different souls in a partnership of equality. And, as modern day women, Eve's relational adeptness is a gift that God continues to bestow upon us.

Based on the work of St. John Paul II, Dr. Savage highlights how women are naturally geared toward relationship:

> In *Mulieris Dignitatem*, John Paul II argues that the feminine genius is grounded in the fact that all women have the capacity to be mothers—and that this capacity, whether fulfilled in a physical or spiritual sense, orients her toward the other, toward persons.[9]

It's interesting to note that Adam is a form created out of matter—which is good, and "Eve is not created out of the same 'stuff' as

Adam—but rather Eve is built (*banah*) out of Adam's rib."[10] Dr. Savage goes on to say:

> There is one remaining element in the Scripture passage that needs to be accounted for, that is, the fact that it is the matter of which man is made that gives of itself for the fashioning of woman. Woman is not created of the same "stuff" as man but "built" out of the man's rib. One implication of this is that it could be said that woman is made from "finer stuff," that is, from matter that already contains a higher degree of actuality and of potency.[11]

When I read that, I thought, "Wow! Could that mean Eve may have capacities that go beyond the matter of which she was made? Capacities that Adam does not have? Knowing women have a deeper sensitivity, could this insight point to the basis of so-called "women's ways of knowing"?

Another author put it this way:

> Here, we are told that God removed a "side" from Adam and "made" Eve. The Hebrew word is *banah*, and it means "to build"... This word comes from the same root as *binah*, which refers to intelligence and an intuitive knowledge of God. In other words, Jewish scholars say, women have been given an extra measure of *binah*.[12]

Bingo! The aha moment arrives. Women have an intuitive sense of the One who is pure love. To me, this intuitive sense points to what could loosely be viewed as "women's intuition." Why do we cry at a Folgers commercial? How can we tell that our child is hurting by simply looking at their face? What prompts us to send a card to a friend we "think" might be struggling? What makes us tilt our head and smile when we hear a newborn baby cry? We do all these things because as women, we have an innate capacity to feel compassion for others. Blessed with an "intuitive knowledge of God," we recognize the power of pure love.

This concept is echoed by Pope Francis in the apostolic exhortation, *Evangelii Gaudium*:

> The Church acknowledges the indispensable contribution which women make to society through the sensitivity, intuition, and other distinctive skill sets which they, more than men, tend to possess. I think, for example, of the special concern which women show to others.[13]

Men, of course, are relationally and spiritually intelligent, too. But they tend to connect most easily with another when they share a common interest or a common goal. Just go to any sports bar during the football season or pick any cul-de-sac in America and watch what happens when one of them brings home a new Harley or a new red Ford F-150. First, there is a lot of peering out windows, and then slowly front doors begin to open, and as if in a trance, men of all ages walk toward the new shiny purchase. Once they get there, they congratulate the new owner, perhaps slapping him on the back, and then a lot of standing, admiring, and much discussion over features occurs. They have connected over their common interest, but this connection won't necessarily lead to a deep relationship where they share intimate thoughts and feelings.

When I was director of community relations for the *Great Adventure Catholic Bible Study*, I created a Leadership Training Day. One of the things we stressed in the training was the value of having separate men's and women's groups. This was never to exclude couples groups—we had many of those—but rather this was done for a few reasons.

First, men and women learn differently; second, men and women share differently; and third, sometimes the men felt like they couldn't get a word in edgewise, especially when they were in groups with women who had the gift of gab. The leadership team soon realized how important it was to give men opportunities to share, with other men, on a deep and spiritual level.

Women, on the other hand, can bond on their way to the ladies' room and end up with a lifelong friend. For example, I met one of my dearest friends a few years ago at a Theology of the Body retreat for teens. I was working at the event, and her daughter was speaking at the retreat. Wouldn't you know, we both heard nature's call at the same time. Once in the ladies' room, we struck up a conversation. It wasn't the fact that we share the same first name (although we do), or that we were both looking for toilet paper that started our conversation. It was the sobbing of a young teenage girl, locked in a nearby stall. As Kelly and I stood at the sinks, washing our hands, our maternal hearts went into high gear. My eyes met Kelly's, and instinctively we walked over to the stall. I knocked on the door and said: "Honey, are you OK?"

Through the sobbing we heard, "I don't know."

Ever so softly, my new friend asked: "Sweetie, can you open the door?"

And slowly the door to the bathroom stall opened, and a tearstained teenager walked into our arms. We left the restroom and found a quiet corner in the church to sit and talk with her. She needed compassion, tenderness, and nurturing. Through tending to her needs, a beautiful, heart-to-heart relationship was born between Kelly, me, and the young teenage girl.

God has given women an innate ability to connect with others. This gift of building relationships was given to women for the greatest of all reasons, to bring others to Christ and build up the kingdom of God. As we build relationships on earth, we are building a communion of hearts. We are connecting ourselves to the Body of Christ. In every relationship, we see a glimpse of heaven.

A woman's intuition is a powerful thing. It must be our extra measure of *binah* that prompts us to share God's love in the world. It's this boundless, irrepressible, radical love that beckons us to feel deeply, care deeply, and connect deeply with others.

SHALL WE DANCE?

The complementarity of men and women and that extra measure of *binah* can be seen beautifully in...Hollywood. I know, right now you're thinking I'm nuts, but hear me out.

A great example of womanhood, as illustrated in the relational beauty of Eve, can be found in *Top Hat,* or *Swing Time*, or *Shall We Dance*, or *Carefree,* or *The Barkleys of Broadway*. Though these movies were made well before my time, I think they offer a modern-day (albeit seventy-five-year-old) picture of the gift of womanhood. The extraordinary success of these movies was not the result of a great script, or even great cinematography. The extraordinary success of these movies was the result of the masterful teamwork of Fred Astaire and Ginger Rogers. I'll even take it a step further and say that in each movie, Ginger Rogers is a perfect example of how a woman's relational genius can complement a man.

Ginger Rogers, the female in this magnificent pair, didn't have to act like Fred to be considered his perfect equivalent. By using her unique and marvelous gifts, she illuminated her femininity and complemented Fred Astaire perfectly.

In fact, Ginger shows how powerful being a woman living your gifts, living your vocation, can be. She didn't look like Fred, and she didn't have to dress like him. (Remember how we dressed back in the 1980s when we wore shoulder pads and business suits to look like men in the workplace?) Ginger was confident in who she was. With grace and elegance, Ginger donned herself beautifully, highlighting her God-given shape, personality, and ability to dance.

And she didn't have to lead because that wouldn't have worked—at least not very well. If you have ever studied ballroom dancing, you know that following is much harder than leading. I learned while talking to ballroom dancers that the reason a woman follows the lead of a man isn't because the man is dominant; it is because women, by their very nature, are geared toward relationship.

A simple Google search on why men take the lead in dancing revealed more about the beauty of the nature of woman in relation to man than I ever imagined. But see for yourself, and read it through your "newly acquired" Genesis 1 and 2 goggles:

> In fact, the leader's part is not that of a ruthless dictator, nor is the follower's part that of an abject slave. In reality in partner dancing, a woman can contribute a great deal to the dance, and a good leader will let his follower shine. People do not like to be coerced, but they do appreciate competent leadership. A good leader will keep the

partnership in synch, but this requires good following. The partnership is just that: a partnership of two people who are equal but different. The woman plays an active role in keeping the partnership together. A man who is coercing his partner into each move, while dancing with a woman who is simply allowing him to do so, will look like a man shaking a rag doll. Watch a good dance couple dancing together and this is not what you will see. Instead you will see two people each bringing their skill to the dance, each working to maintain the partnership, and each having fun.[14]

The relational woman appreciates a good leader, someone who understands what a true partnership looks like. Fred Astaire knew that he and his dance partner were an equal team. He always kept Ginger before him, meeting her gaze. Ginger Rogers knew the importance of being Fred's helper (*ezer*). She was always in tune with his steps and could foresee the glides and twirls that were coming. Using her intuitive senses, she followed him gracefully. And the two became one in a masterful display of dance that generations continue to celebrate.

Ginger Rogers and Fred Astaire shared a beautiful partnership. Hollywood didn't need to tell us that—we knew it "from the beginning." The book of Genesis told us: "So God created man in his own image, in the image of God he created him; male and female he created them" (Genesis 1:27). God created men and women to complement one another, to reflect each other's pure beauty. And what is pure beauty, pure love? It's the dance of the Father, Son, and Spirit—the Trinity reflected in our lives. It's God in three persons at work in us.

The example of Fred and Ginger is a beautiful illustration of the creation story. Men and women were created differently but equally. Bestowed with radical relational abilities, women are built with an extra measure of *binah*. We follow the lead of our intuition and our steps are aligned with the heartaches and joys of others. We recognize pure love and beauty when we see it. With well-tuned hearts, we celebrate the dance of Father, Son, and Spirit.

Tools for Building Your Relationships
Scripture

Read the second account of the story of creation in Genesis 2:20–23, and then read it again more slowly. Then read it for a third time noting the words or insights that jump out at you. Write down those words and the thoughts you had about them.

Meditation

Prayerfully consider a partnership you have with a man, be it a romantic relationship, a marriage, or a partner in a project. List the feminine traits that make you a suitable and therefore a desirable partner in that relationship.

Questions for Reflection and Discussion

1. In Genesis 2:20–23, we learn that there was no suitable partner for Adam, and so God formed a woman from the rib of the man. Why do you suppose God chose this place (versus clay or dirt) to form a woman?

2. What changes in the relationship of Adam and Eve when we say Eve is created "last" instead of "second"?

3. Can you think of any appealing TV commercials, movie scenes, or song lyrics that present the radically relational gift of

women? What was attractive or especially appealing?

4. By creating and participating in cooperative relationships, men and women display a powerful human connection to others who observe them (just like Ginger and Fred). They display human relatedness itself as an attractive reality. How might you use this insight to change how you participate in relationship with your husband or another male figure in your life?

5. How can you invite others to create (or renew) their own relationships through your example?

LIVING YOUR RELATIONAL GIFTS

Option 1: Choose someone with whom you have a close relationship. Decide to invite them to a special encounter: a meal, a day or afternoon visit to a place or an event, something that would be special to you both. Because you know this person well, what will you do and how will you prepare for this encounter to protect and deepen your relationship? Include some way to connect spiritually as well as on the friendship level.

Option 2: Choose two of your family members or friends who are close to you. Take some time alone, reflect on those friendships, and then, write a thank you note to Jesus for your special gifts and talents for relating to others, which have developed and sustained these relationships. Thank him also for whatever in these relationships has brought you closer to him.

PART TWO

*The Bridge from
Heart to Heart*

CHAPTER FIVE

Relating Heart to Heart

If it hasn't happened to you, you've seen it happen to someone. You're sitting in Mass, perhaps caught up in the beauty of what is happening on the altar, perhaps distracted by the artistic Cheerio display the toddler in front of you is creating, and in an instant you could be the grand prizewinner on *Name That Tune*. Why? Because with just three notes you immediately recognize the song about to be sung—it's the song they sang at your loved one's funeral. You begin the fight to hold back the tears. Usually, this is a battle lost midway through the first verse.

For many, the song of heart-rendering recall is one such as: "On Eagles Wings"; "Here Am I, Lord"; "Amazing Grace"; "How Great Thou Art"; or "I Am the Bread of Life." You probably are saying the name of your total-recall song in your head right now. For our family, it is "We Remember (How You Loved Us)" by Marty Haugen.

The summer before my senior year of high school, my Auntie Lani was diagnosed with ovarian cancer. This was an incredible blow to our family. Lani was thirty-eight years old, the baby of eight kids (a surprise pregnancy for my forty-two-year-old grandma, but a very welcome surprise), and truly, she was the life of the family. She was the pulse that kept our family beating as one.

Lani was the planner, the organizer, the creator, the entrepreneur, and the comedian all rolled in one. She would gather the family for any occasion, and if there was not a true occasion, she'd make one up. Once she decided that she wanted to go to the Kentucky Derby, but since she had neither the means nor the time, she cooked up a scheme to bring the Kentucky Derby to Minnesota.

Now, one would think that if you wanted to bring the Kentucky Derby to your neck of the woods you'd just watch it on television, or perhaps place a bet and share a Mint Julep or two with your friends. But not Lani—to her that would be dull, and besides, she had the idea in June, so waiting until the following May just would not do!

To her, it made total sense to recreate the entire Derby. Her recipe was simple: invite the whole family to your little house in Roseville, Minnesota. Divide one bocce ball court into six lanes. Take six nieces and nephews, put numbers on their backs, and place them on six stick horses. Acquire two large dice and one vintage Chuck-a-Luck metal dice cage. As guests arrive, have the family members you have roped in as volunteers greet them and hand out laminated cards of the Minnesota Derby rules and regulations. When you want to announce the beginning of the races, simply blast "My Old Kentucky Home" over your 1982 JVC Ghetto Blaster Boom box, and then prepare for "The Most Exciting Two Minutes in Sports"…or the most ridiculous two hours in family history.

If you were one of the fortunate six to jockey a stick horse that day (and I was lucky number 5), you only moved ahead one foot (on the sixteen-foot bocce ball court) when your number was rolled on the die. With all the shenanigans and comical color commentary, this race lasted well beyond two minutes. I don't remember who won. It might have been my cousin Jenny or my brother Jim, but I do remember the crowd—they were unruly! But what made them unruly was the amount of laughter that permeated the air in our backyard Churchill Downs. All this happened because of one joy-filled woman who loved her family.

Lani was diagnosed with ovarian cancer on her thirty-eighth birthday, August 14, and went home to be with Jesus just eight months later on April 3. My mom pulled me out of school for two weeks in late March of my senior year to be with my family, but most importantly to spend time with her baby sister who was my mentor, my idol, my everything. I was so blessed to spend Lani's last two weeks on earth with her, something I am eternally grateful to my mom for allowing me to do.

Lani's love for her family was only overshadowed by her love for Jesus. Rarely did a visit go by where she didn't pull her guitar from her red Chevy Celebrity and gather all the nieces and nephews around her so she could teach them a song that praised the Lord. I guarantee that, if any of my cousins are reading this book, right now they are all singing, "Do Lord," and hearing Lani's voice chime in with, "Oh Lordy."

Lani was a musician and cantor at her parish, and she planned her own funeral. A week before she died, I was in her room with my aunts—Linda, Sr. Pat, and Sr. Paula—as Lani was sitting on the edge of her bed singing the songs she wanted played at her funeral Mass.

"Here Am I, Lord" was sung with the most sincere of hearts and brought tears to my eyes. But it was when Lani sang, "We remember how you loved us, to your death, and still we celebrate, for you are with us here…" that something happened inside of me I will never forget. I remember thinking, *I wish this moment would last forever. I don't want you to be just a memory. I can't live with you being just a memory.* Suddenly, the reality of losing her hit my seventeen-year-old heart, and I began to sob.

Just nine days later, we sang, "We Remember" at her standing-room-only funeral, and believe me, there wasn't a dry eye in the house. In the years to follow, whenever the song "We Remember" was sung at Mass, you could watch our family drop like flies in the battle to hold back tears, and I was always the first to lose.

Then one day, after crying for nine years every time I heard that song, things changed. It was the morning of my nephew's baptism. My brother had given us fairly good directions to the church, which was two hours away, but we—his wonderful side of the family—all got lost. Luckily, as we entered Mass *very* late, a kindly usher said he would assist us to find a spot where we could all sit together. This was wonderful, since the six of us (my mom, dad, sister, husband, myself, and our two-month-old daughter) were embarrassed and didn't want to make a big scene.

The usher proceeded to walk us all up to the front row on the left side of the altar. (Perhaps this is why Catholics always sit in the back pews, so they can laugh at those who come in late and are placed in the only remaining spot, the front row!) My brother, who was sitting front and center with his wife's family (who had all been on time), instantly shot us the "are you kidding me?" look. Fabulous! All eyes *were* on us, but that attention seemed to be short-lived, for soon it appeared the congregation had forgotten about our grand entrance and was now focused on the celebration of the Eucharist. Praise God, our moment in the spotlight had come to an end...until they played the Communion song. Hearing just three notes, I could name that tune, and I began a whole new prayer, "Please, Lord...please...please, don't let me lose it."

I imagine my prayer was heard, but it was not quite answered the way I had hoped. Midway through verse one the tears started rolling down my checks. My mom was the next to lose that battle of the tears. She began crying during the second chorus, and by verse two my sister had joined us. As we rustled to find tissues, we noticed my brother looking at us across the church, and by the third chorus he was crying with us. Then, the choir went on to verse three, and I thought, "I don't ever remember more than two verses to this song." We all continued to cry and once again, all eyes were on the crazy disruptive family in the front row. By the fifth time we heard the chorus sung, my mom leaned over and through tearstained eyes said, "How the hell many verses does this song have?"

That did it—we lost it! My sister and I broke out in the worst case of church giggles ever and couldn't stop laughing. Though we tried, we simply couldn't stop. Our shoulders were shaking as we tried to keep our laughter under control. But the musicians continued to repeat the chorus two more times.

I turned to look at my brother. He was shaking his head, no doubt totally embarrassed by his family. But there was a smirk on his face; I know he was thinking the same thing we all were thinking: "Dang you, Lani...you made us laugh again!" My aunt's love for us reached down from heaven. It was a moment of unexpected grace, a union of hearts. Our sadness quickly turned to joy.

RADICAL LONG-DISTANCE RELATIONSHIPS

During my eighteen years of Catholic schooling, I had never ventured into the book of Revelation. To me that book was filled with terrifying images of the end of the world and was something Catholics just didn't read. It was a book for Protestants, Hollywood, or Kirk Cameron to interpret—or so I thought.

But as I've continued along the path of Scripture study, I've discovered that this apocalyptic book contains a message of hope for all believers. In the pages of Revelation, we are reminded that in the Mass, heaven and earth become one. Each time we gather to celebrate the Eucharist, we are truly united with those in heaven—we are connected with all those who have gone before us and now live in the light of the Beatific Vision. How cool is that? We are mystically connected with our loved ones in heaven and all the saints with them! This is the communion of saints.

We, the Church, are a communion, a communion of those who have died and are being purified, those who are saints in heaven, and those of us who are pilgrims on earth. How cool is that? We are in union with those who have died and are being purified; these are the souls in purgatory, souls that we pray for. We are in union with the blessed in heaven; these are the saints, the souls standing before God. These are the souls who we ask to intercede for us. They are before God and offering up prayers for us to God. In Revelation we read: "And another angel came and stood at the altar with a golden censer; and he was given much incense to mingle with the prayers of all the saints upon the golden altar before the throne; and the smoke of the incense rose with the prayers of the saints from the hand of the angel before God" (Revelation 8:3–4). And we are in communion with each other in the communion of faith, for our faith is a treasure in life that is enriched when we share it. We are united to each other through the sacraments, through our charisms and through charity (see CCC 950–953). This is the mystical body of Christ. What a radical exchange between earth and eternity!

Though it may seem like we are separated from those who have died, and our grief may at times overwhelm us, our connection to them must not be classified as a long distance relationship. Think of it this way.

You are at Mass, and at the moment when the priest says: "Lift up your hearts," and the congregation responds: "We lift them up to the Lord," heaven and earth become one.

As you look around, you see every space in the Church, every inch of every pew, every aisle, every area around the altar occupied by hundreds of saints. Instantly you recognize well-known saints like St. Francis, St. John Paul II, St. Mary Magdalene, and the Blessed Mother. Perhaps you see hundreds who are not known to the world. Then, in a moment of indescribable joy, you see the saints you know well—those whose loss you have grieved: your mother, your brother, your daughter, your husband, your grandpa.

Imagine the excitement you would feel standing beside your patron saint or your confirmation saint! Imagine the incredible joy in your heart knowing you are being reunited with your loved ones! You are in communion with them. It is a bond that is beyond earthly realms, stronger than the bonds of any friendship. It is a mystical bond from heart to heart—a communion of souls. It is the joy of being in the body of Christ.

The Church teaches:

> We believe in the communion of all the faithful of Christ, those who are pilgrims on earth, the dead who are being purified, and the blessed in heaven, all together forming

one Church; and we believe that in this communion, the merciful love of God and his saints is always [attentive] to our prayers. (CCC 962, quoting Paul VI, Credo of the People of God § 30)

To think that the saints are *always attentive* to our prayers is something in which we should take great comfort.

I imagine I'm like many other women; much of my time is spent attending to the needs of others, and I am often overlooked unless there is a lost baseball uniform that needs to be found in the next thirty seconds, a treat that must be baked for the bake sale that morning, the latest iPod that a child must have or he'll no doubt be the "laughing stock of the sixth grade," or a house that needs to be cleaned and a gourmet dinner that must be whipped up in forty-five minutes before my husband comes home with his clients from out of town. So to think that the saints are always attentive to my prayers is somewhat humbling. *Who, me? The saints are praying for* me? To know that someone is in the presence of God and does not cease to intercede for me is beyond amazing!

As women, we should be calling upon the saints constantly! Given our natural orientation to others, the saints will help us build holy relationships within our families, our friends, and our community. They will lead us to those who need Christ. Most importantly, they will help us find union with God.

CELESTIAL SIGHTINGS STRENGTHEN THE HEART
Union with God: The saints are praying that we find it. But in our busy, everyday lives, it is sometimes hard to imagine that the God of the universe is truly with us. We are consumed with bills we sometimes cannot pay, illnesses that have no cure, or brokenness

that seems impossible to be healed. Though busy and at times stressed, we may feel that our little humdrum lives don't merit any attention, especially not from a God who has greater things to attend to, such as hungry children in Africa or good people being persecuted for their faith. It is at times like this that I am reminded of some of the best advice I ever received when I doubted my importance to God. I was telling a beautiful religious sister that I felt almost guilty asking God to answer my prayers when others were in much greater need than I was, and with her tender smile and sweet southern accent, Mother Assumpta said to me, "Honey, God loves to be God. It's his job, and he's good at it. You just pray to him and let him do his job. You'll see, he'll show you that he is listening."

Mother Assumpta was right. Every now and then, God checks in with us in big way. He gives us glimpses into the joy that awaits us in heaven. I call them celestial sightings—little snapshots of God's grace. Luckily for us, these inspiring images come in a variety of sizes: 4 x 6, 5 x 7, and 8 x 10.

The 8 x 10s are the big glimpses of heaven we receive through the sacraments, sacred Scripture, and sitting before the Blessed Sacrament. You might remember being taught that the sacraments are *visible symbols of God's presence.* They are outward signs of inward grace, which means that the sacraments bring the grace of God into our souls. *God with us!*

> The sacraments of Christian initiation—Baptism, Confirmation, and the Eucharist—lay the *foundations* of every Christian life.... By means of these sacraments of Christian initiation, [the faithful] receive a measure of the divine life and advance toward the perfection of charity. (CCC 1212)

What could be a more perfect example of the union that awaits us in heaven than to have God dwelling within us on earth!

Sacred Scripture could be compared to a photo album of 8 x 10s —big, clear images of our destination. Throughout Scripture we are constantly directed toward union with God. In the Old Testament, the people of Israel struggled to obey God, to have a binding relationship with him. In the New Testament, Jesus brings us into that binding relationship, the New Covenant, and in doing so, he points us to eternal life with God. I think one of the best glimpses of the glory that awaits us in heaven is the transfiguration (see Luke 9:28–43).

To set the stage, knowing that Peter, James, and John were going to experience Jesus's death and crucifixion and had a road of incredible confusion, temptation, and fear ahead of them, Jesus takes the three apostles up Mount Tabor where they are given the greatest of all mountaintop experiences. As Jesus was praying, "the appearance of his countenance was altered, and his clothing became dazzling white. And behold, two men talked with him, Moses and Elijah, who appeared in glory" (Luke 9:29–31).

What a sight to behold! Peter is so caught up in the glory of the moment that he doesn't want to leave the mountaintop. Can you blame him? He's experiencing a huge glimpse of heaven! He is seeing two of the greatest leaders of the Jewish faith before him, and he's witnessing his friend's appearance completely change and radiate with the glory of God.

Though I heard this story many times, one day while reading my Bible, the meaning of it really hit me, and I was left sitting in awe. On that particular day, I suddenly realized that Jesus comes to all of us in our smallness and gives us incredible moments of insight that help us strive for heaven—*especially* when we feel like throwing in the towel. In fact, as I read the response of Peter to what he was experiencing, an image came to my mind that made me laugh and allowed me to relate to Peter as just a normal guy. When Peter sees this marvelous scene coming to a close, he says to Jesus, "Master, it is well that we are here." I love that. How simple, how true, and how so like I probably would respond to seeing something so magnificent. I can totally picture Jesus turning to Peter, looking at him with the corners of his mouth turned up, raising one eyebrow, and saying, "Ya think?"

Pope Benedict XVI once said, "There is nothing more beautiful than to be surprised by the Gospel, by the encounter with Christ."[15] That day, a Scripture I had heard so many times surprised me! That day I encountered Christ in a big 8 x 10 celestial sighting. Now, I look forward to the surprises of insight I find in the pages of Scripture, and I encourage you to do the same. Pick up your Bible, open it up to a familiar story, and as you read it, use the eyes of your heart to see what God is showing you to help you at that exact moment in your life...and know, whenever you are reading the Bible, Jesus is saying to you, "[Your name], it is good that you are here."

8 x 10 moments

The 5 x 7s are our awakening moments. They are the times when we are deep in prayer and can hear the voice of God. They are the highs you feel working in your gifts, or the joy that comes with knowing you are part of something bigger, something greater—you are a part of the body of Christ and you are using your gifts to build up his body. Have you ever experienced a time where you instinctively knew what to do—you knew how to do it, but you didn't know why you knew those things? And then after

5 x 7 moments

you did it, you felt great. You knew your actions had been a positive contribution. Those are moments of awakenings that bring with them a wonderful joy.

I remember the first time this happened to me. I was asked to be the emcee at a prominent Catholic school gala. I had never spoken in front of a large group, much less been the one who set the energy of the room and moved the pace along. Why I was asked, I have no idea. In fact, I don't even know why I said yes. Actually, my honest and superficial reason for saying yes at the time was because the event was six months away and I figured standing up in front of five hundred people would be just the inspiration I would need to get in shape. Though I had half a year to get in shape, I didn't—but God didn't care what shape my body was in; he was working on my soul. God showed me that night that he had given me a gift to build up the kingdom.

With much preparation and twice as much prayer, I emceed the event, and it was a blast! I seemed to know exactly what to say and when to say it. The night moved along with great energy and much laughter, and the school accomplished the goal it had set. At the end of the night I was overcome with this great sense of joy, thrilled that I could play a part in something so meaningful. As my husband and I drove home, I sat in awe of all that had happened. I reflected on the comments people made about my skill in speaking in front of a large group and my ability to motivate people. It was a 5 x 7 moment for me. For the first time in my life, I considered that perhaps God was calling me to build up his kingdom by speaking in front of people and sharing my joy. Now I know that the internal happiness I experienced as I recognized a gift God had given me for the good of his kingdom was only a foretaste of that which we all will experience in heaven.

The 4 x 6s are our God-incidences—coincidences that have the hand of God written all over them. You can probably think of ten right now that have happened to you in the past month. For me, one particular God-incidence comes to mind.

On New Year's Eve, each person in our family randomly picks a saint to be his or her patron saint for the year. One year, my saint was Mother Teresa of Calcutta, so I decided I would try to emulate her love and complete sacrifice for the Lord. But mind you, I was going to ease into it; there would be no boarding a plane for India, yet.

As I was driving to work one morning, I was talking to Mother Teresa and telling her my plan. I told her I wanted to have that *deep thirst* that she had for Jesus, but I was scared. For some reason I feared I would obtain the thirst, and then just remain, well, thirsty. At that exact moment, a truck merged onto the highway right next to me. It was so close to me that it startled me, and I turned to look. It was a huge delivery truck painted with the most beautiful and realistic mural on it. The mural was of huge water droplets and across the top of the truck were the words, "Quench Your Thirst!" I just smiled and said to my new cohort for the year, "OK, Mother Teresa, I want you to help me thirst for Jesus."

If you can't think of a God-incidence now, don't worry. I'm trusting that in the next few days you'll be thanking the Lord for sharing a little 4 x 6 picture with you.

Of course, there is also the wall mural, the greatest snapshot of all: The Mass! It's the ultimate picture of the communion that awaits us. Heaven and earth kiss, and we receive the Body and Blood, Soul, and Divinity of our Lord!

Sometimes, God gives us multiple snapshots at once, a kind of cosmic collage, to really encourage us along the way. I have no doubt that my nephew's baptismal Mass was just that. On that day, in her own special way, my Auntie Lani played a huge part in healing our hearts. On earth, she wove our family together with laughter and love. From heaven, she turned our tears into joy. She was created for relationship. And I know, beyond a shadow of a doubt that it wasn't just a coincidence that "We Remember" was sung at Communion—that was a high-res 4 x 6 if I ever saw one.

Tools for Building Your Relationships
Scripture

Read the words of Ruth to Naomi in Ruth 1:16, and then read it a second time more slowly. Then read it for a third time noting the words or insights that jump out at you. Write down those words and the thoughts you had about them.

Meditation

Remember a time when you felt great devotion in a relationship. What caused you to feel such deep devotion toward the other person?

Questions for Reflection and Discussion

1. Recall a special event or time with your extended family. What do you remember most about it? Was there anything that happened that united the family in a special way, or something that challenged their unity instead at that time? Share how you might pray for the people in your family who were there at that event or time.

2. Think of that moment in the liturgy when we are surrounded by the communion of saints. Name the saints you know, name the

persons in your family who have gone before you, and name the persons in your family you know will want to be there. Which saints do you turn for intercession and spiritual friendship? For which of the persons in your family do you pray in spiritual friendship?

3. How has the reading of this chapter changed your understanding of the relationship of Jesus and his Mother? Revisit the 5 x 7 mysteries of the rosary. Review the 8 x 10 events in the Gospels where we hear about Jesus and Mary. What stands out in their relationship? How might this change your prayer to Mary to intercede with Jesus for you?

4. Did any 4 x 6 "coincidences" with God occur to you while you read this chapter? Share one in your journal—or, if you are reading this with a group, with the members of your group.

5. As women, we seem to find it natural to enter into the lives of those around us who are suffering. Can you describe an example of this from your own life experience, or have you recognized this quality in someone else—perhaps a friend?

LIVING YOUR RELATIONAL GIFT

Option 1: Go to the grocery store. Pick out a single flower (it doesn't have to be a rose, but roses are special). Take it to a weekday Mass or to a place people go to pray. Present it to someone with this greeting: "This is from St. Thérèse, the Little Flower. She wants to befriend you. Here is a prayer to her." Hand the person a card with the following prayer:

Most gracious Little Rose Queen, remember your promises of never letting any request made to you go unanswered, of sending down a shower of roses, and of coming down to earth to do good. Full of confidence in your power with the Sacred Heart, I implore your intercession in my behalf and beg of you to obtain the request I so ardently desire: (mention it). Holy "Little Thérèse," remember your promise "to do good upon earth" and shower down your "roses" on those who invoke you. Obtain for us from God the graces we hope for from His infinite goodness. Amen.

If this seems too daring, then simply leave the flower and prayer in the pew. Whether you hand it to someone or leave it in the pew, remember to pray for the new friend of St. Thérèse all that day. And remember; now *you* are a special friend of St. Thérèse for introducing her to a new friend!

Option 2: Is there a song, a hymn, a recited prayer, or even a special sacred art piece that speaks to you and moves you to tears, or turns your heart to God in a powerful way the moment you see it, hear it, or talk about it? Whatever that special encounter is or when it occurs, God's desire for you and your desire for love have met. Write the words or paste a picture in your journal. Speak to the living God who knows you so well that he gave you this special moment so you will know how much you long for him.

CHAPTER SIX

A Personal Approach to Sharing Your Faith

I travel a lot for my work, and as such I spend many hours on planes flying from sea to shining sea. I always pray for the person I am going to sit next to on my flight...for many reasons. On one particular day I was flying from Minneapolis to New Jersey to speak at a women's evening of reflection put on by my sister in Christ and partner in evangelization, Patti Jannuzzi. I was looking forward to a night of music, inspiration, and adoration before the Blessed Sacrament. "There will be wine and cheese after your presentation," Patti had said. *Cool!*

As I sat on the plane reviewing my notes, I struck up a conversation with the middle-aged man sitting next to me. As is common airplane chatter, I asked him where he was heading. Was New Jersey home for him? In an instant his eyes grew wide, and he shifted toward me and excitedly said, "I'm going to Jersey to open a kosher Mexican restaurant."

I tilted my head in confusion. He enthusiastically went on to tell me how he had eaten at one in Los Angeles and couldn't wait to bring this idea to Jersey. My mouth dropped open as questions filled my mind. *How do you serve kosher food if you can't serve meat and dairy together? Mexican food has about five ingredients made in different (and delicious) configurations, but still, two of the ingredients are cheese and sour cream. And the major ingredient is meat! Is there a big Latino Jewish community that I'm unaware of?"*

Trying not to look too perplexed, I listened as he began sharing his story with me—his ideas, his hopes, his fears, and surprisingly, his religious beliefs. He was a Jewish man who loved his faith and his God.

He admitted to falling away from the traditions of his family, but a gentle smile came across his face as he spoke of what Passover meant in his house when he was a child. Then, after a while, he looked at the Bible sitting on my tray table.

"What do you do for a living?" he asked.

I smiled. "I traveled the country teaching people how to put on Catholic Bible studies."

This was turning into a conversation I never saw coming.

"So, you're Catholic then?" he said.

"I am..."

There was a long, drawn-out silence.

"Can I ask you some questions?" he asked.

At that moment, a prayer rose up inside of me, unbidden: *Come, Holy Spirit. Give me the words. Give me the courage. Give me the wisdom to answer this man... Come, Holy Spirit.*

"Sure." I replied.

"On television or in movies, I always see Catholics praying the rosary. What's that all about?" he asked.

I began explaining, "The rosary is a beautiful repetitive prayer that helps you meditate on the life of Christ. As we say the prayers in repetition, it's almost like we are breathing, and it helps us focus on Jesus. And as we pray, we ask Mary, our Blessed Mother, to intercede for us."

He responded, "Well, why do you do that? Why do you seek Mary's intercession? "

I looked at him with a little smile and said, "Hmmm, kind of because of you."

"*What?*"

That caught the attention of some of the surrounding passengers, and ears perked up as they began to listen to our conversation.

I continued: "You see, back in the time of King David, the queen was never the wife of the king. The king had seven hundred wives and three hundred concubines. Had the king named one of them queen, there would have been a big catfight at the palace."

He laughed.

"In the time of King David, the queen was always the mother of the king. In Hebrew, she is known as the *gebirah*, the mighty woman, and if you wanted something, you didn't go directly to the king; you went to his mother to intercede on your behalf (see 1 Kings 2:13). That's why we go to Mary, because she is the Queen Mother. She will always intercede on our behalf. She will bring our needs to her Son," I said.

He looked at me like a three-year-old who just learned the greatest secret and said in a drawn out way, "Cool!"

"I know," I replied.

"OK, I have another question," he said. "Why do you listen to some white-haired guy in Rome? Why do you let him tell you what to do?"

And I replied, "Well...that's because of you, too...kind of."

Now he was really intrigued. Eagerly, he leaned in to hear the explanation. Feeling as if the Holy Spirit was hovering above us, I continued:

"Back in the time of King David, when the king had to leave the kingdom, he would literally give the keys to the kingdom to the prime minister and put him in charge. In Hebrew, it is the *Al Beit,* the one over the household. Now, fast-forward a thousand years or so to Caesarea Philippi when Peter declared that Jesus was the Christ. Jesus said to Peter, 'Blessed are you, Simon Bar-Jona! For flesh and blood has not revealed this to you, but my Father who is in heaven. And I tell you, you are Peter, and on this rock I will build my Church, and the gates of Hades shall not prevail against it. I will give you the keys of the kingdom' (Matthew 16:17–19). And every one of the apostles was blown away, because they knew exactly what just took place! Jesus had given Peter the keys to the kingdom and made him the *Al Beit.* At that moment, Peter became the first pope, and the Catholic Church can trace her roots through the succession of the popes, all the way to Jesus. It is what we call apostolic succession. In fact, if you ever see a statue or painting of St. Peter, he usually shown with the keys."

My seatmate looked at me with awe and said, "That is so cool!"

"I know!" I replied.

Then I said, "Want to know something about our Mass on Sunday?

"Sure."

"It is deeply connected to the Passover."

"No way! How come no one ever told me that Catholicism and Judaism were so closely related?" he asked.

As the plane landed and we were getting ready to deplane, he said, "Kelly, can I ask you one more question?"

I laughed and said, "Why not? You're on a roll."

He grew somber and said, "You're the first Christian who hasn't told me that I am going to go to hell because I haven't accepted the Lord Jesus Christ as my Lord and Savior. Why didn't you try to convert me?"

"Because that's not my job," I answered. "I'm called to share the truth of Jesus Christ. And, I know with all my heart that God sent his only begotten Son to earth, who humbled himself to become one of us, suffered with us, died among us, and rose from the dead so that I could go to heaven and you could go to heaven. My job is to share the message of Jesus Christ with you and pray for you to come to know Jesus."

I paused and then continued, "It's not my job to convert you. It's the job of the Holy Spirit to convert the heart and if he fails he can take it up with the 'Big Guy' upstairs."

He gave me the biggest smile and thanked me for my enthusiasm and passion for my faith. As he walked away, he squinted his eyes and looked at me intently.

"Are all Catholics like you?" he asked.

To which I replied, "Yes," with a wink and smile.

"Right," he said with a laugh.

And all the passengers within earshot chuckled, too.

Now, of course, I know all Catholics aren't like me, and so did he. But if all Catholics made the commitment to share their faith, imagine what could happen! Hearts would be transformed. The joy of the Gospel would be shared, and relationships with Christ would be nurtured.

Five years have passed since that encounter on the plane. Since that time, I've come to understand that our call to evangelize others doesn't need to be complicated. We don't need to hand out *Catechisms* to everyone we meet. We don't have to speak eloquently about the Lord. We don't need to pursue a theology degree or know how to teach. And we don't need to feel that we are responsible for the conversion of another's heart. All we need to do is call on the Holy Spirit. No matter who we are, he can work through us to bring another person to Christ. We just need to share our story of faith. That's how we "make disciples of all nations" (Matthew 28:19).

As women we are equipped in a special way to evangelize the world. God has given us a natural orientation to others. We've been blessed with intuition. We are attuned to the voice of God.

COME, HOLY SPIRIT

"Come, Holy Spirit." Can you imagine what might happen if every Catholic woman in the world prayed this simple prayer? Surely, we would become evangelists, eager to share our faith with all. In essence, we would *be* what we should *be*...and we would set the world on fire!

All Catholics could be like this, eager to share their love of the Lord with others. Some just don't know it yet because they haven't had a personal encounter with the Jesus Christ. Some lack the confidence to do it. But once a heart has been transformed by an encounter with Jesus, the joy of the Gospel takes over and there arises an intense thirst to go deeper in that friendship with the Lord and a hunger to share the joy with others. As we nurture that relationship with Christ, we become passionate about sharing our Catholic faith.

EVERYDAY CONVERSATIONS FROM THE HEART

Pope Francis recently told us, "Dialogue is much more than the communication of a truth. It arises from the enjoyment of speaking and it enriches those who express their love for one another through the medium of words."[16]

During that plane ride, at 33,000 feet in the air, a Jewish man and a Catholic woman both thoroughly enjoyed speaking to each other, and both walked away enriched by the experience. Why? Because we shared our stories. I loved hearing about the kosher taco shop that he wanted to open in New Jersey. He heard about my love for Jesus and gained new perspectives—not only about Catholicism, but also about his own Jewish faith.

Though I had never met the man, the Holy Spirit had prompted me to pray for him even before I boarded the plane. How could I have known that he was looking for answers about Mary, Jesus, and the Catholic Church? But the Holy Spirit had prepared me well. In the years leading up to that encounter, I had heard Jeff Cavins teach in depth about the *gebirah* and the *Al Beit* and the Gospel of St. Matthew. I knew those Scriptures well, and now I was teaching people how to lead fruitful Bible studies. That day on the plane, I had everything I needed: a listening ear, an understanding of the Scriptures, and most importantly, the power of the Holy Spirit.

When we open ourselves up to the Holy Spirit, radical things can happen. Who knows, perhaps the Jewish man was radically changed by our interaction. Perhaps, after he started his Kosher Mexican restaurant, he gave his life to the Lord. Ah...such wishful thinking. I may never know how things worked out for him, but what I do know is that God blessed our conversation, and that's enough for me.

The best way to evangelize, as Jesus modeled for us, is to share the Gospel with a personal approach. For example, let's say you want to talk about the totally awesome things Pope Francis is saying about evangelization. If you say to someone, "Have you read the apostolic exhortation, *Evangelii Gaudium*?" you are most likely going to get an, "Evang-gel-lililiy Gawd-e-what?"

But if you say, "Hey, did you hear about the great letter by Pope Francis called *The Joy of the Gospel*?" you are probably going to get a, "No, what does he say in it?"

In *The Joy of the Gospel*, Pope Francis tells us that there is a kind of preaching that is the responsibility of all of us. He reminds us to share our faith in a way that "is always respectful and gentle." And that "the first step is personal dialogue, when the other person speaks and shares his or her joys, hopes and concerns for loved ones, or so many other heartfelt needs...."[17]

Our Holy Father also calls us to remember that "only afterward is it possible to bring up God's word, perhaps by reading a Bible verse or relating a story, but always keeping in mind the fundamental message: the personal love of God who becomes man, who gave himself up for us, who is living and who offers us his salvation and his friendship."[18]

Jesus commissioned *all* who believe in him to make disciples of all nations, but he did not leave us on our own to do it. Matthew 28 ends with Jesus saying, "And behold, I am with you always, to the close of the age."

If God's Spirit lives within us, we will always be led to those who need Jesus. As faith-filled women, attuned to the voice of the Spirit, we can share the message of God's love and salvation with boldness. Our relationship with the Holy Spirit will grow every time we say yes to his voice and promptings. If we ask for the help of the Holy Spirit as we share the message of God's love, evangelizing others, we need not be afraid of saying the wrong thing. The Holy Spirit will give us courage, confidence, and just the right words.

THE JOY OF EVANGELIZING

Ironically, I never set out to "evangelize" anyone. Like most women, I simply love to hear a good story. And I love to share my own stories of family, work, and faith.

Though the settings and scenarios may differ and the conversations vary greatly from person to person, a few key items remain consistent in my sharing of the Gospel message. I hope these ideas are helpful to you:

Ask the Holy Spirit to help you. Pray: "Come Holy Spirit!"

Listen to people. Try to hear their hopes, their pains, their concerns for loved ones, their needs. You'd also be surprised how much people will tell you when you are sitting at a baseball game, or waiting for a bus, or shopping for groceries!

Share your story, your joys, and your struggles. Don't feel as if you have to have all the answers. A person who is willing to be a bit vulnerable is much more relatable than a "know it all."

Talk about your relationship with the Lord. Be joyful. Laugh with the other person. Mention the ways in which you've grown in relationship to Christ, but be sensitive to the individual's journey of faith. Perhaps quoting a Bible verse won't be as important as simply being present to him or her.

Let the Holy Spirit handle the conversion stuff. Thank the Lord for the opportunity to share his love.

Each encounter is different. Sometimes I invite the person to pray with me and assure him or her of my prayers. Sometimes I give the person a good resource that fits his or her needs, or we become Facebook friends. And sometimes we go our separate ways. Whatever happens, you can be sure of this: When you plant a seed of faith, God will send someone else to water, fertilize, and tend the soil that surrounds that seed.

Today, decide to be a relatable woman. Share the good news of Jesus with those you know well and those you've just met. Turn your ear to their stories. And with great joy, share yours. Lean in and listen well. Be a voice for Christ at the grocery store or the doctor's office or in the air. You've been created to share his love.

Tools for Building Your Relationships
Scripture

Read more about the Samaritan woman encountering Jesus as she went to draw water from the well in John 4:25–29. This time, prayerfully read how Jesus "evangelizes her" and how she tells others. Notice that her immediate reaction was to pass on this amazing news. Read the verses again, more slowly this time. Then read it for a third time, noting the words or insights that jump out at you. Write down those words and the thoughts you had about them.

Meditation

If you were to have an "encounter at the well" with Jesus, who would you most want to go and tell?

Questions for Reflection and Discussion

1. Have Catholic friends, non-Catholic friends, or even strangers asked you about aspects of the Catholic faith? Pick two or three aspects you don't know much about and research the answers. The *Catechism* is a great place to start, and you can also find good information on the Internet—check out Catholic

websites such as www.catholic.org or www.newadvent.org. Your local Catholic bookstore also has a wealth of resources. Come up with a question someone might ask you, and prepare a response. Compare your response with someone else in your group.

2. Among your acquaintances, are you aware of one or two who are lacking in confidence about sharing their faith with others? What might change that reluctance and shyness into bravery? More importantly, what plan of action might you take to assist that change? If *you* are the reluctant one, what will it take to change you?

3. A personal encounter with Jesus Christ is an amazing experience. It enlivens the Christian faith, increasing hope and love through a more active participation in the sacraments. Can you identify a moment in your recent past when you felt much closer to Jesus than usual? With whom did you immediately want to share that experience of closer relationship with Jesus?

4. When we speak or write, we reveal ourselves even without realizing it. It's this personal approach that draws others toward us. What do others think about your faith? Do they recognize your deep relationship with the Holy Spirit? Do they see you as a disciple of Christ? Do you think your excitement and joy in Jesus draws them to the faith?

5. Do you know your story about your relationship with Jesus the Lord well enough to tell it briefly and joyfully? Get that story ready to tell someone. Do you pray for everyone with whom you have a conversation? Begin today with an easy prayer: "Holy Spirit, bless this person I am speaking with. Let me be a blessing to him or her."

LIVING YOUR RELATIONAL GIFT

Option 1: Share the JOY! Download and read a copy of *The Joy of the Gospel* (available free at http://w2.vatican.va/content/francesco/en/apost_exhortations/documents/papa-francesco_esortazione-ap_20131124_evangelii-gaudium.html). Tell five of your friends individually that you have read it, and share with them what about the Gospel makes you especially joyful. Ask each friend to share with you what makes him or her joyful about the Gospel of Jesus Christ.

Option 2: Make a list of opportunities you encounter in a two-day period to meet someone new (whether you take advantage of the opportunity or not). Such opportunities are all around you: the person behind you in the supermarket checkout line, the salesclerk in a store, or someone you've never spoken to as you exit Mass. Ask yourself if there might be a way to connect and say something positive (however small) about faith, Jesus, love, or joy. Make a note of what to say next time (it might help to write it down).

CHAPTER SEVEN

The Visitation—A Perfect Example

Late one April I received a phone call asking if I'd be willing to give a talk on Mary, the Mother of God, and the New Evangelization. Instantly I answered, "Yes!" I love talking about the Blessed Mother. Luckily, the talk was scheduled for September at a parish about ninety minutes away. No problem—that gave me an entire summer to write a talk. I decided I'd get through the rest of the school year with the kids, and come June 4, I'd sit down and write my talk.

Well, June came...and June went. Suddenly, before I knew it, the kids were climbing back on the bus for the first day of school, and I hadn't written a thing. No problem—the house would be quiet, and I could spend the next three weeks concentrating on my talk.

I've got to write that talk. It's really getting close, I told myself a week before the talk. By now you've probably realized that I am really good at the art of procrastination. On the morning of the presentation, I came up with a foolproof plan. I would drive down to the church with my friend Cathie, hand her a piece of paper and a pen, and with my hands on the steering wheel, she would jot down my thoughts for the presentation.

My plan to write on the run didn't unfold as I thought it would. On the day of the presentation, as Cathie and I drove through the freeways of Minneapolis, we talked and laughed and caught up with each other. But by the time we headed into the rural country-side, the biggest storm I'd ever seen was rolling in.

All cars were forced to pull off to the side of the road as a wall of clouds turned into a funnel cloud turned into a tornado. At that moment, I uttered one of my most heartfelt prayers. "Dear Lord, do not let me die in Zumbrota, Minnesota!"

Well, God didn't let me die. (Thank you, Lord!) But needless to say, my talk didn't get written. No problem—there was another speaker, Brother Chris Alar, speaking before me, so I figured while he spoke, I'd just pray to the Holy Spirit for some much needed inspiration. "Give me the right words," I whispered.

THIS LITTLE LIGHT OF MINE

What I forgot was that Br. Chris is an on-fire, engaging Catholic speaker. A few months earlier, I had worked with him on the creation and promotion of the *Hearts Afire Parish-Based Programs for the New Evangelization*. On multiple occasions, I had heard him share his love for the message of Divine Mercy and his devotion for our Blessed Mother. He's like the energizer bunny on an I.V. drip of Red Bull. Like all the people who filled the pews around me, I was captivated by his presentation.

Br. Chris was talking about the shroud of Turin. He explained that in the late seventies or early eighties, two scientists by the names Jackson and Jumper conducted an intensive research project to prove the shroud to be either real or a hoax. Br. Chris went on to say that the scientists had used a VP8 image analyzer, which is an analog device that converts image density (lights and darks) into vertical relief (shadows and highlights).

A hush fell over the room as Br. Chris said that the research team concluded that the image on the shroud was not something drawn or painted, but rather that of a "real human form of a scourged, crucified man." All eyes were fixed upon Br. Chris. "The image on the shroud was caused by a sudden and intense burst of light," he said with incredible passion.

Walking back and forth on the stage, he said: "Don't you get it? That was the resurrection! Jesus is the Light of the World, and at that moment of the resurrection... *Bam!* The Light of the World shone like never before!"

As I sat there, taking it all in, I felt my own "Bam!"—a bright light went on in my head. Once again, the Holy Spirit had heard my cry for help, come to my aid, and given me an instantaneous insight.

I was barely introduced when I leapt on stage and matching Br. Chris's enthusiasm, immediately said, "That's what we need! Don't you see? That's what we all need! We all need to be that burst of light that radiates Christ to the world!"

As I spoke, thoughts were popping into my head faster than I could have ever imagined, yet they were coming out of my mouth in clear, intentional sentences. It was surreal. All at once a sensational excitement had come over me, yet at the same time I was filled with tranquility and peace. I can only describe it as an "electrifying comfort." I was being hit with a sudden burst of the Holy Spirit. *Bam!* At that moment I became a vessel, a conduit for the message the Lord had for all the people who had braved the storm to come to the church that night.

As I spoke, a quote by Madeleine L'Engle came to mind. "We draw people to Christ...by showing them a light that is so lovely that they want with all their hearts to know the source of it," I shared with the crowd.[19] I could barely contain myself. The Spirit was moving. "Do you know what that light is? It's the key to evangelization! It's joy! If you want to lead someone to Christ, then radiate his joy! Shine with a joy that is so enticing that people want what you have!"

J.O.Y.

When I was in eighth grade, we got a new principal, Sr. Mary Gwendolyn. At the end of every single day, over the P.A. system, Sr. Mary Gwendolyn said the same thing to us: "Remember children, Jesus, others, then yourself. If you put your life in this order: Jesus first, then Others, then Yourself, you will have JOY."

Back then, it was a little annoying to hear this day in and day out. But now that I am older, I see the wisdom of this good Franciscan sister. When our relationships are ordered in such a way that we put God first, we will know true joy.

Joy isn't merely a happy feeling—a feeling of contentment when everything is going perfectly in life. If this were true we would probably never know true joy, because each day we are faced with unexpected interruptions, frustrations, heartaches, and challenges. It's hard to imagine feeling completely content when the phone won't stop ringing, or traffic is causing you to be late for an important meeting, or your laundry room is filled with suds because your eight-year-old decided that if "Dawn cuts through grease," it surely would be able to clean his jeans. If we based our happiness on our circumstances, we'd probably be a very unsatisfied crowd.

Some people think that joy is something that we can gain on our own accord. We think, *I'll be happy when I get a bigger house, a better car, a perfect job, more money….* OK, it doesn't take a rocket scientist to prove this notion false. In fact, a green Grinch shows us every Christmas that no matter how much "stuff" we acquire (or in his case, steal), we can never acquire true happiness. Remember that story? Though he stole everything from the Whos in Whoville, it was only when the Grinch heard the Whos singing that he realized their happiness was not a result of possessions. And once he realized this, his heart grew three sizes. When the Grinch saw that the Whos had true happiness, then he *truly* wanted what they had! He wanted joy. For us, that joy is God dwelling within our souls.

Cardinal Timothy Dolan once tweeted, "Joy isn't some giggly, Pollyannaish mania. Those people get on your nerves. Joy is interior peace that gives rise to exterior happiness."[20] In other words, joy is the light that radiates from our faces when we know that our relationship with God is a forever one. It is the light we've been called to pass on to others.

A RELATIONSHIP BETWEEN TWO WOMEN: THE ULTIMATE EXAMPLE OF EVANGELIZATION

In the joyful mysteries of the rosary, we see an example of how we should bring Jesus to others—the visitation—that is worthy of our reflection.

Imagine what it must have been like for Mary on the day the angel Gabriel paid her a visit (see Luke 1:31–33). Mary, a young girl of about thirteen years old, awoke to find an angel in her room. As if that isn't enough, the angel told her she was going to have a son—she would conceive of the Holy Spirit, her baby would be the Son of the Most High, he would be a king in the line of David, he would reign over the house of Jacob forever, and his kingdom would have no end. Wow! I'd say Mary had a pretty big morning! And what is the first thing she did? Did she complain? Call her friends and say, "I can't believe this is happening"? No. She went in haste to visit her cousin Elizabeth because the angel told her that Elizabeth, in her old age, was six months pregnant.

We don't know for sure why Mary left "in haste." Perhaps Mary, so sweet and humble, went to Elizabeth in haste because she was drawn to help her older cousin in her time of need. Imagine Elizabeth's situation. She's "advanced in age," pregnant with her first child. Any woman who has been pregnant in her twenties or thirties knows the toll a pregnancy can take on a young body. Just imagine being pregnant in your older, frailer years.

Perhaps she went in haste because she was overcome with an uncontrollable eagerness to share the joy and awe of that which was happening within her with one who could understand; she knew that Elizabeth would be able to relate to what she was experiencing.

Whatever her reason for going in haste, Mary met Elizabeth where Elizabeth was at on her journey in life. She brought new life to Elizabeth—a much older cousin who had been barren her entire life and was living in the hill country of Judea.

Have you ever felt like Elizabeth? Have you ever felt as if your time of great conversion has passed, that you have nothing to give, that you are living in the hills of loneliness? Maybe you've had moments, as I have, when you feel isolated from God.

Mary immediately shared with Elizabeth what she has received; she shares Jesus. By simply being present to Elizabeth, she is saying: "We will walk together in our journey of faith. We will share our stories, our hearts, and our yes to God. As friends, we will come to know our Lord and Savior."

In our modern lives, Mary enters into the same kind of relationship with us. She is a wonderful example of a radically relational woman and mother. She is the great evangelizer, always drawing us into a personal relationship with her Son. I find myself wanting to emulate her love of Jesus and her willingness to be guided by the Holy Spirit. Like her, I long to trust in the will of the Father with all my heart. But, let's face it: Mary's got one up on you and me—she was born without original sin. Yet Mary hastens to be at our side, to put us in the presence of her Son, to help us say yes to the will of the Father. At the moment when Mary shares what she has received with Elizabeth, it's as if she takes her *fiat* (her "yes" to God) and makes it our *fiat*. Mary invites us into her yes. She assures us of her motherly tenderness and nurturing, and she encourages us as we say yes to a life with Christ. And, as a good mother, she leads us by example, showing us how to live the will of God and how to bring Christ to the world.

In the scene of the visitation, Mary modeled perfectly how we should bring Christ to others. What was the first thing Mary did when she completed the rigorous journey up the hillside to Elizabeth? Did she collapse in a chair in Elizabeth's house, throw her feet up, and say, "Wow, am I exhausted from that little hike!" No! She shares her JOY. The first thing that radiates from Mary is her joy. Mother Teresa said, "Joy was the Virgin's strength. Only joy could give her the strength to walk without getting tired up to the hill country of Judea in order to carry out a servant's work."[21] When Mary finally arrived at Elizabeth's home, she was so full of the joy of the Holy Spirit that she not only radiated it, she couldn't contain it. She burst into song:

> My soul magnifies the Lord and my spirit rejoices in God
> my Savior. (Luke 2:46–47)

How does a mouth magnify the Lord? It's simple. You just need to say, "Lord, you are magnificent." But how does a *soul* magnify the Lord? The soul magnifies the Lord by radiating the joy of Jesus. The busy young mother who takes time to help a stranger in dire need to find her boarding pass radiates the joy of Christ. The woman who pours her heart into organizing and enthusiastically inviting people to a Bible study radiates the joy of Christ. The person who sends you a text message, just when you need it, just to let you know you crossed her thoughts and she is praying for you, radiates the joy of Christ. The smile and wave of someone you accidentally cut off in traffic radiates the joy of Christ. Joy is radiated when love shines through any circumstance.

Mary's joy is uncontainable. As she continues singing the song that welled up in her heart, she tells Elizabeth what God has done for her. She shares her story, her encounter with the Lord.

> For he has regarded the low estate of his handmaiden. For behold, henceforth all generations will call me blessed; for he who is mighty has done great things for me. (Luke 2:48–49)

Then, Mary's joy-filled hymn becomes the ultimate praise and worship song:

> And holy is his name. And his mercy is on those who fear him from generation to generation. He has shown strength with his arm, he has scattered the proud in the imagination of their hearts, he has put down the mighty from their thrones, and exalted those of low degree; he has filled the hungry with good things, and the rich he has sent empty away. He has helped his servant Israel, in

remembrance of his mercy, as he spoke to our fathers, to Abraham and to his posterity forever. (Luke 2:49–55)

In her shout of praise, Mary tells Elizabeth who God is. In sharing Jesus with another person, we are called to do the same. We are called to tell who Jesus is.

SIMPLY TELL OTHERS WHO HE IS

When I was working on my master's degree, I took a class called "John Paul II and the New Evangelization." After an in-depth study of the Acts of the Apostles, my classmates and I were all on fire with a renewed zeal to proclaim the Good News. One day, we were given the assignment of evangelizing someone. Prior to hitting the road, we met in small groups to discuss the best way to go about sharing the Gospel. One gentleman in my group came up with a plan: "OK, so we find someone and then give them the *kerygma.*"

Now, for those of you who haven't brushed up on your Greek since your sorority days, the *kerygma* is the initial proclamation of the Gospel. Simply put, it is the message that Jesus Christ, through his life, death, and resurrection, gained salvation for us. It is the message that we are loved and saved by God!

Upon hearing this plan, I called out: "No way! We pray!" (Sometimes I lack a holy filter, I know.) God bless my classmates! They had to listen to my rant, which went something like this: "We don't just find someone and give them the *kerygma.* We pray. We pray that the Holy Spirit will lead us to the right person. We pray that we will be given the right words. We pray for the wisdom and the courage to proclaim the Gospel. We pray that the love of Jesus will reach out to that person long after his or her interaction with us."

Luckily, the man who had offered the "plan" must have been more amused than offended, because he laughed and gave me a hearty, "Amen, sister!" From there our small group entered into a lively discussion about how and why we are called to evangelize.

At the visitation, Mary uses simple words to tell Elizabeth who God is. In the power of the Holy Spirit, she sings his praises. With great joy, she tells her cousin that God is holy, strong, merciful, and faithful. If we look at Mary's interaction with Elizabeth as a perfect example of how we can share Christ with others, then Mary telling Elizabeth who God is would be like us sharing who Jesus Christ is.

The visitation is a perfect example of how we can share Christ with the world. First, we must shine with the light of Christ. Then, we need to charitably meet people where they are at in their spiritual journey, listen to their stories, and share ours. We can tell them how Jesus Christ has changed our lives, just as Mary told Elizabeth what God had done for her. Then, as Mary did at the end of the Magnificat, we can tell them who God is! We can tell them who Jesus is! That's sharing the *kerygma*.

WOMEN AS EVANGELIZERS

Women have been created to relate. Reaching out to others comes naturally to us. So why does the thought of evangelizing someone scare us so much?

Perhaps our hesitation is rooted in our sensitivity to others. We don't want to be too pushy. We want to respect different political views and religious affiliations. Maybe we feel insecure about our lack of theological training. Maybe as Catholics we feel that talking about a personal relationship with the Lord is reserved for our Protestant brothers and sisters.

At the visitation, Mary reminds us that we have been created to relay a message of hope to others. Mary shows us that we can and should proclaim Jesus as Lord, even if we think it may be a wild and foreign concept to someone. Imagine how wild it sounded when Mary finally got around to telling her extended family members that the Holy Spirit overshadowed her and she was going to be the mother of God! I'll admit, there have been times when I've been hesitant to share the Lord with someone because the words "politically correct" crossed my mind. It is at times like this that I pray with fervor to the Holy Spirit to give me the right words.

I always want to be charitable and respectful, but at the same time, how can I love my neighbors and not share with them the way to salvation? When I do so, I am almost always amazed by their response.

Another time when I was once again at thirty thousand feet in the air, I began talking with a beautiful woman about her faith. She asked me if I had accepted the Lord Jesus Christ as my Savior.

"Yes, absolutely; I'm Catholic," I said.

She went on to say that she "used to be Catholic," but now she had found a spiritual home in another denomination. She loved her church so much that she then tried everything in her power to get me there.

"We have amazing programs, awesome sermons, and fabulous music," she said.

I was truly delighted with her excitement.

"You should consider leaving the Catholic Church," she said.

In that moment, something overcame me. I guess I got a little choked up because my eyes began to water, and I softly said, "I wouldn't leave the Eucharist for anything."

Her bubbly excitement changed.

"I wish I was that convicted about my faith," she said with sincerity. Now her eyes were misting too.

"You can be," I told her.

I took the chance and shared the truth about my faith. I relied on the Holy Spirit, and I shared my convictions with all my heart. In doing so, I was able to give a sister in Christ a beautiful new look at Jesus and his Church. I believe I was able to do this because I allowed the Holy Spirit to work through me, and because I have a wonderful model when it comes to proclaiming the faith with conviction, confidence, and hope. I have the Mother of God. Mary gives us a perfect example of how we are to share Jesus with others, how to evangelize the world.

THE SPIRITUAL TOOLBOX

We have quite a mission, don't we? Fortunately, God has given us a spiritual toolbox filled with tools that will help us share his love. He has given us the Holy Spirit, sacred Scripture, and the sacraments (especially the Eucharist). The more time we spend listening to him through the Scriptures, talking to him in prayer, and receiving him in Holy Communion, the closer we will become to him.

So, how is *your* relationship with Jesus? Do you call him a friend? Do you spend time with him each day? Are you aware of the ways in which he is working in your life?

One of the best ways to build a strong relationship with the Lord is through the practice of *Lectio Divina. Lectio Divina* is a method of prayerfully reading sacred Scripture in which you slowly read, meditate, pray, contemplate, and respond to a specific verse or verses in the Bible (often the Psalms). It a wonderful habit to get into. In this ancient form of prayer there are four steps: *lectio*, where you read the verse slowly; *meditatio*, where you reflect on what you have read and on what God is saying to you; *oratio*, where you respond in prayer from your heart; and *contemplatio*, where you let go of all your thoughts and ideas and simply rest in God's presence.

For example, let's take a moment and prayerfully read the beginning of Mary's beautiful song of joy, the Magnificat. Begin with step one, *lectio*, and read the following out loud slowly: "My soul magnifies the Lord and my spirit rejoices in God my Savior" (Luke 2:46–47).

Now read it again, slowly, and then once more, this time listening to the words or phrases that jump out at you. As I read it just now, "magnifies the Lord" and "spirit rejoices" are capturing my attention.

Now, on to step two, *meditatio*. Mediate upon those words that caught your attention. You may want to consider all the meanings of the word *magnify*. You might meditate on what it means for your spirit to rejoice. Perhaps times in your life when you were so filled with happiness that your spirit rejoiced might fill your mind. What did that look like?

Next is your time to respond to God. This is step three, *oratio*. You might ask the Lord, "Lord, when has my soul magnified you?" Or you might say, "Lord, help me rejoice in the simple knowledge that you are my Savior."

Finally, enter into *contemplatio* and contemplate more deeply the meaning of what the Lord is saying to you right now. Listen to the sound of his voice. Let your own thoughts go and just rest in the Lord. Perhaps during this *contemplatio* time, a sense of complete peace and joy will fill your heart, like it did mine.

You may want to try practicing *Lectio Divina* each day. It's a wonderful way to enrich your faith life and familiarize yourself with the beauty of God's word.

As you continue to build your relationship with Christ, keep your spiritual toolbox open. Inside, you'll find amazing tools to help you build the body of Christ, such as prayer, the Holy Spirit, *Lectio Divina*, and the sacraments—most importantly, the Holy Eucharist. When you are nourished with the Bread of Life, Christ himself, it's easier to share him with others. Remember, Mary carried the Bread of Life within her womb for nine months, and then in her heart forever. She was sustained by the presence of Jesus, and we must be, too. Why not add daily Mass to your weekly routine? An hour before the Blessed Sacrament will provide untold strength for your personal journey of faith. When you carry the Lord in your heart, as Mary did, you'll not only be able to share him with others, you will overflow with eagerness to do so.

The Source of Our Joy

Imagine for a moment that you are witnessing the visitation. You see two women jubilantly run toward each other, their arms outstretched. As they embrace one another, you witness their excitement and hear the unmistakable sounds of laughter, joy, and song. These two women are friends, sisters in Christ. Their lives are connected by the unfolding plan of God.

Mary and Elizabeth share a radical bond. Through the message of an angel and by the power of the Holy Spirit, these women have gone from being merely kin to being sisters in Christ. In the Visitation, we witness the beautiful joy-filled embrace between the one bearing God and the one supporting the God-bearer. Here we rejoice in what it means to bring Jesus to another, and we learn what it means to embrace and support each other on this journey. Here we see that each of us can bear Christ to the world through what we share and how we receive that, which is shared with us. No matter what hillside we live on, each of us has a role in bringing Christ to the world. All we need to do is let the light of Christ in our hearts radiate so brightly that people cannot help but to want to know with all their hearts the source of our joy.

TOOLS FOR BUILDING YOUR RELATIONSHIPS
Scripture

Read Luke 1:39–45 and notice how Elizabeth shares in Mary's *fiat,* and then read it a second time more slowly. Then read it for a third time, noting the words or insights that jump out at you. Write down those words and the thoughts you had about them.

Meditation

Close your eyes and replay this scene in your imagination. What particular detail about this encounter stands out to you? What might the Holy Spirit be showing you?

QUESTIONS FOR REFLECTION AND DISCUSSION

1. Can you remember a time when you put off a responsibility until "the moment of truth" was upon you, and you had to turn to Jesus to ask for help? Describe the details of the situation. How did Jesus help you? (And how long did it take you to thank him?)

2. Was the phrase "Jesus, others, and you" new to you? How does that pattern apply to your family and friend relationships? Does putting Jesus first, then others, and yourself last fill you with joy, or does it seem burdensome? What action can you take today to put JOY back in your relationships?

3. In his post-synodal apostolic exhortation On Catechesis in Our Time (*Catechesi Tradendae*), Pope John Paul II tells us that people hear and receive the good news more readily from the witness of others.[22] Can you reveal some significant encounters with people when it was so easy to speak of your experience with Jesus?

4. Go through your spiritual toolbox given you by the master craftsman: God the Father. What do you find in there? Which sacraments and what Scriptures provide you with strength and strategy for sharing your life in Christ with others?

5. When we go out to eat, we choose the foods we like from a menu. We also pay attention to calories and the nutritional content of the food. Which of the nourishing tools the Lord has given us are on your regular diet? Specific prayers? Scripture-reading sessions? Daily prayer? Volunteer work at the parish? Where do you find Jesus offering you his support and nourishment on the road of evangelization?

LIVING YOUR RELATIONAL GIFT

Option 1: Write out the Magnificat and pray it with your name in it. For example, "Suzy's soul magnifies the Lord...." Do this for a week and record what happens in your relationship with the Holy Spirit.

Option 2: This week, make a visit to a parish you don't usually attend for Sunday liturgy. Spend time before Mary's shrine within that church. Ask her to introduce you to the Holy Spirit. Be specific about your request to her: Tell her you want the gifts of the Spirit for evangelization. Which ones do you think you need the most? Fortitude? Wisdom? Knowledge? Fear of the Lord? Something else? Ask Mary to show you where you need the Holy Spirit to "overshadow" you for magnifying the Lord.

PART THREE
Finding Your Balance

CHAPTER EIGHT

Letting the Peace of Christ Rule Your Heart in a World That Wants to Rule You

On a cold, wintery Minnesota day, a friend invited me to speak at a women's evening in Clearwater, Florida. The answer to that invitation was a no-brainer—*yes*! It was one of those Holy Spirit invitations. The topic was the role of women in the New Evangelization, and here's where the Holy Spirit comes in.

CHRIST-CENTERED CHAOS

My friend had no plan, no location, and she was caring for her husband who had terminal cancer—but she wanted the evening to happen in three weeks! Her life, as she knew it, had been tossed into turmoil since Mark, her love of forty-seven years had received the devastating terminal diagnosis; yet she had heard the voice of God telling her to gather women together at this moment in time. Years of listening to the Lord and speaking with him led her to know that she had best respond to his call.

What occurred next was amazing. Carol and the Holy Spirit put together an incredible night. Everything fell into place perfectly. A beloved priest in the community, Monsignor Toups, returned from speaking to all the bishops that morning at the USCCB gathering in California and was able to begin the evening with Mass. Amazing musicians offered their time and talent. Four hundred women from around the diocese came together on short notice to laugh, cry, and learn of their beautiful role in evangelization. That evening the seed of a new and exciting ministry for women was planted. All of this was impressive, but what truly impressed me was what was going on behind the scenes. I can honestly say I have never seen such chaos!

Carol's husband was in the end stages of cancer. He was being cared for in their home, which now contained a hospital bed, a shelf of medications, and caregivers around the clock; yet Carol had graciously invited me to stay in the guesthouse on their property. From the moment I entered their house I could sense a tangible peace, although their lives were in complete upheaval.

Days before the women's evening, a huge tree had fallen in Carol and Mark's yard, barely missing the house. The night of the event, a pipe burst, causing irreparable damage to the walls and the floor of the room where Mark lay in his hospital bed. Everything had to be moved, gutted, and repaired. I have never seen so many workers go through a house in such a short period of time. No sooner would one leave than another would show up. We even joked that it would be the perfect place for a single woman to meet a man because there were so many of them stopping by!

Somehow in all that chaos, in the swirling of the door as a plumber left and a carpenter appeared, there was a noticeable calmness. It was there because Mark and Carol's home was centered on Christ. Jesus was the calm in the whirlwind.

Every person who entered Carol and Mark's house that day encountered Christ, and I was blessed to be able to watch it. Carol spoke to workers about their lives and openly talked about Jesus. Mark's room was adorned with objects of his faith, and his eyes and voice were as gentle as one would envision the eyes and voice of Christ to be. The caregivers served him with joy. Kids and grandkids came in and out. Friends stopped by unexpectedly and happily learned they arrived just in time to move Mark's hospital bed into Carol's office. Later that evening, it was Carol's office that became a worship space as Msgr. Toups and Fr. Malley celebrated the Holy Eucharist.

PEACE IN TIMES OF SUFFERING

I think back to that twenty-four-hour period often, especially when I find my life spinning out of control and feel like I can't find peace. Carol and Mark remind us that peace is the hallmark of a true relationship with Christ. In the forty-plus years that preceded Mark's diagnosis of cancer, Carol had met the Lord in Scripture, meditating, contemplating, and listening to the sound of his voice. She had built a radical relationship of trust and confidence in God.

We all long for peace, especially when our lives are filled with unrest. I remember sitting in class one day toward the end of my senior year of college and being completely overwhelmed by the thought of all my finals, finishing and presenting my thesis on genetics, creating a resume, and finding a job. I remember thinking, *Once I get past May, my life will be calm.*

Exactly two years later I was planning my wedding, finishing nursing school, getting ready to take my nursing boards, working two jobs, and coaching volleyball. *After the month of May, everything will be OK,* I thought to myself.

This cycle of longing for peace in the midst of chaos continued on for years as I hauled three kids to and from every event under the sun, volunteered for a multitude of causes, and tried to juggle a career at the same time. But you know what? It was never getting through the proverbial "Mays" in my life that helped me find peace. Only when I made a deliberate effort to be quiet and still, to be alone with God, did I find the peace that I was longing for.

That message continues to speak to me today. I've learned that the quiet peace of Christ can easily be hidden in the noise that so often fills our life. I think of the disciples caught in the storm at sea (see Mark 4:35–41). Imagine the frightful sounds they heard: the wind howling, the waves crashing against their boat, the sounds of their own fear-filled screams. The storms of life are loud, aren't they? When we face uncertainty, it's hard to ignore the thundering voice of fear and the crashing waves of doubt. But in these frightful times, Jesus promises to come to us. When we give him our trust, praying and meditating on his Word, he will calm our hearts. Even when we are drowning in a swirling sea, he will say, "Peace, be still."

PEACE IN THE MIDST OF PAIN

There was a time when I was going through some serious moral suffering. After experiencing an unexpected betrayal, I was inconsolable. My husband and close friends were at a loss at how to comfort me. I finally hit rock bottom. It was two o'clock in the morning, and I was lying on my living room floor sobbing—and I mean *sobbing*! I was a mess—literally! I had mascara running down my cheeks, hair hanging in my face, and tears dropping onto my shirt. This wasn't a pretty, soap-opera cry.

My spirit was crushed, my heart broken. I couldn't pray. In fact, I didn't want to. Talk about not wanting to relate to God! "Jesus, I trust in you," I heard myself say. But no sooner had I said this than the thought hit me: "Lord, I don't know if I *do* trust you." In my brokenness, I wasn't even sure of God's presence.

At that moment all I could do was turn to my Blessed Mother and ask her to help me—to help me trust her Son. I kept saying over and over, "Mary, you stood at the foot of the cross and watched your Son die and you still trusted in the will of God. Help me trust." After several minutes, the tears stopped, my breathing settled, and a peace came over me. I was still in pain, but my doubt in God was subsiding. As I pulled myself up onto my couch, it was as if I experienced the comfort of crawling up into my Mother's arms, and I curled up and fell asleep there, picturing myself on her lap, wrapped in her mantle.

Have you ever experienced this kind of suffering? Maybe right now you are facing a great physical or financial struggle or a huge, life-changing decision. If you are grieving a loss, you may be having a hard time getting up in the morning. Anxiety can cause all sorts of physical symptoms, from headaches and stomach pain to ongoing fatigue.

Pope John Paul II called it the "pain of the soul."[23] This type of anguish cuts to the core. It's more painful than childbirth. (And for me to say that speaks volumes of the anguish endured; I have no pain tolerance when it comes to physical pain. In fact, I almost named my first child epidural, as I thought it was the closest thing to heaven I had ever experienced.)

As I faced the "pain of my soul," the next day I sought the guidance of a dear friend of mine, Fr. John Klockeman. After hours of crying, talking, and praying, he left me with some advice. He said, "I want you to cling to John 20:11–18." He opened his Bible and began to read about Jesus appearing to Mary Magdalene outside the tomb. I left his office with an armful of wet tissues, red, puffy eyes, and a holy reading assignment. For the next few weeks, I faithfully read the Scriptures he gave me over and over throughout each day.

After weeks of reading, all I could think was: "Why am I reading this? Mary Magdalene doesn't seem to be of any help. My heart is still broken. My spirit is crushed." I would fall asleep crying and wake up with the feeling of pure emptiness and start crying again. *What is the point of this story?* I kept wondering.

Then, one day, the veil lifted. As I imagined Mary Magdalene standing at the tomb, I boldly asked her: "How is it that I spent all this time with you in the pages of sacred Scripture and in prayer and yet I feel like you are not with me?

Suddenly, I made a connection I had never before seen. In her darkest hour, when her Lord, her hope, her Savior was dead and buried, Mary Magdalene went to the tomb. She went to where she knew the Lord to be. And it hit me—she had led me to do the same.

In the pain of my soul, I had gone to daily Mass, and I had cried my way through every reading, response, and hymn. Day after day, I had been given strength and comfort from the Holy Eucharist and the sacrament of confession, receiving untold graces. With diligence, four times a week I sat before the Blessed Sacrament. I never left singing "Zip-a-Dee-Doo-Dah," but I did find comfort there, crying before my Lord. Many times a day I read and meditated on John 20:11–18. And I prayed without ceasing. In my darkest hour, Mary Magdalene had led me in her footsteps. Like her, I had gone to where I knew Jesus to be.

Mary Magdalene had a beautiful relationship with Jesus. Like every woman, she was created to relate to her God. She was oriented to him and trusted him completely. What a beautiful example she provides to those who are facing trials! As she persevered through her suffering, she was greatly rewarded. She was the first (besides our Blessed Mother, according to the Church Fathers) to see the Risen Lord! And she was the first one to proclaim his resurrection to the world. "I have seen the Lord!" (John 20:18).

On that day outside the Lord's tomb, Mary Magdalene became the apostle to the apostles. As I continued to reflect upon her story, I kept reading one passage over and over again: "But Mary stood there weeping" (John 20:11). One day, through my laughter and tears, I cried out, "Lord, I can do that! I can stand here weeping, Jesus, *and* trust in you!" At that moment, I encountered the greatest peace I have ever known: God's peace; God's presence in my pain.

PEACE IN UNEXPECTED PLACES

The Hebrew word for peace is *shalom*. However, *shalom* is a word that means much more than the mere definition of freedom from disturbance. In his article *A Primer on Peace*, Msgr. Stuart Swetland writes: "'Peace' is a biblical term. In the Old Testament, the Hebrew word for peace is *shalom*. Literally, it means 'to be complete or whole.'"[24]

Shalom is used in many different ways in the Old Testament. It can mean general prosperity or well-being (see Genesis 15:15; Psalm 4:8); safety or success (see 2 Samuel 11:7; 18:29); harmony among friends and family members (see Zechariah 6:13); and harmony among nations (see 1 Kings 4:24; 5:12). When used as a greeting or as a blessing (as it was and still is used by Hebrew speakers), it conveys the notion that one is wishing *all* good things to the person addressed (see 2 Samuel 15:9). Simply put, though the word *shalom* carries multiple definitions, it finds its essence in the root verb that means to be complete and whole.

That's a good question.

So what makes you feel complete and whole? Do you need to feel as though you are in control, that you have a plan for your life, in order to feel secure? Do you need to be healthy, strong, or financially stable to obtain the perfect peace of Christ?

Mother Teresa taught us that sometimes the peace of Christ can be found in imperfect places. In the streets of Calcutta, in the poorest of poor, she saw Christ. In the physically and emotionally straining work of caring for the unwanted, unloved, and uncared for, she tended to the needs of her Lord. When she served the poor, the neglected, and the sick and the dying, she served Christ.

Like Mary Magdalene, Mother Teresa went to where Jesus was. In the pain and suffering of others, Mother Teresa found her savior. She knew that relating to God's people with love and compassion was the key to letting Christ's peace rule in one's heart.

THE SIMPLICITY OF PEACE

God doesn't demand perfection from us. On the contrary, he promises us his peace in the most painful, confusing, and imperfect moments of life. In St. Paul's Letter to the Philippians, he wrote, "Have no anxiety about anything" (v. 6), but he didn't stop there. Instead of just encouraging words, he continued to give guidance on how we can be anxiety free. He says, "But in everything by prayer and supplication with thanksgiving let your requests be made know to God," and he shared what the outcome will be if we follow his advice: "And the peace of God, which passes all understanding, will keep your hearts and minds in Christ Jesus" (Philippians 4:6–9).

So how do we experience the peace of Christ in our lives? We completely trust God for *everything,* and we strive for that which makes us complete and whole. St. Paul gave us insight into how we can rely on God for everything, but what makes us complete and whole?

The *Baltimore Catechism* gives us some insight into this question. If you were lucky enough to go to a Catholic school between 1895 and the late 1960s, the odds are you have the answer to this question memorized. Let's try it. See if you can answer question six of the *Baltimore Catechism* before reading the answer.

Q. Why did God make you?

Don't look! What's your answer?

A. God made me to know him, to love him, and to serve him in this world, and to be happy with him forever in heaven.[25]

That's it. The answer is simple. Our happiness, our peace, and our completeness can only be found *in* God.

LET THERE BE PEACE ON EARTH

I once had the privilege of being present at a talk given by Father Jacques Philippe. Through a fabulous interpreter, I heard his powerful message. He said that if you are troubled by anything, you have not completely abandoned yourself to the will of God. He went on to explain that abandoning oneself means that one recognizes one's smallness, one's powerlessness. Only when we realize that all the good we do comes from God can we obtain true peace of heart.

Ironically, the timing of Fr. Philippe's talk perfectly coincided with a decision I needed to make regarding my career path. (Of course, I realize this wasn't ironic timing at all for God!) I thought

I had given my decision to God. But I was still trying to control the direction of my life, weighing the pros and cons of each job, without seriously considering that God held the reins concerning my future.

That night, as I drove home from the talk, I prayed: "Help me abandon myself to your will, Lord." Later, when I fell asleep, I closed my eyes and smiled. For the first time in weeks, I felt at peace. The next day, the Lord showed me exactly which path to take, and there was no mistaking his sign—it was accompanied by a feeling of great confidence.

I would recommend Fr. Philippe's book *Searching For and Maintaining Peace* for any busy woman to keep in her purse or diaper bag. Fr. Philippe uses the words of a holy, courageous businesswoman, Marie of the Incarnation, who founded the Ursuline order in New France, to describe the perfect peace of Christ:

> If we could, with a single interior glance, see all the goodness and mercy that exists in God's designs for each one of us, even in what we call disgraces, pains and afflictions, our happiness would consist in throwing ourselves into the arms of the Divine Will, with the abandon of a young child that throws himself in the arms of his mother.[26]

Most mothers can relate to this powerful image. In fact, I can still remember the look of peace on my son's face as he faded off to sleep in my arms late one night. Looking at my little preschooler sleeping so peacefully, one would never guess that just minutes earlier, he had been awakened by a nightmare. With fear in his eyes, he had burst through our bedroom door, bolted toward our bed, and thrown himself into my arms. He knew that here he would be safe from the monsters that had scared him in his dreams. In my arms, he would find peace.

Right about now, some of you might be thinking, *I'm going through the worst experience of my life. I'm sorry. I don't feel any peace at all.* Just so you know, you aren't alone. Everyone feels this way at one time or another. Even the king of Israel experienced this.

In the book of Psalms, David cries out to the Lord to come to his aid, and he does not mince words. In fact, in Psalm 12, he begins with a simple, "Help, Lord…" Throughout the psalms, David pleads with the Lord to rescue him. When he abandons himself to the Lord completely, God does not disappoint. The peace of God sustains David and strengthens him to persevere in God's plan.

Like David, we are called to trust in God. But life is filled with hard things. Each day we encounter barriers to trust. If we have been lied to by a loved one, or gossiped about, it's difficult to get past the hurt we feel. It's easy to blame God for the inevitable heartaches of life. If we experience a job loss or some other unexpected change or trial, we can start thinking that God has forgotten us. We can experience a deep anxiety that isolates us from the Lord. And our relationship with Jesus can suffer greatly.

But the Scriptures tell us: "Have no anxiety about anything" (Philippians 4:6). Like King David, we can call out to God in our troubles. Sometimes, all we need to say is: "Help, Lord." It's a small but powerful prayer, and it always moves the hand of God. What a powerful relationship we have with God! In him we find our help and peace.

GRACIOUSLY GRANT US PEACE

A couple years ago, at the wedding Mass of a good friend from high school, my family was sitting next to some friends of ours. I was sitting next to a member of their family who was Lutheran, and as we were leaving the church he asked, "How come Catholics never completely finish the Lord's Prayer?"

I looked at him and said, "What do you mean?"

He replied, "You stop before you say, 'For the kingdom, the power and the glory are yours, now and forever.'"

Instantly an insight filled my mind and a smile graced my face. I said, "Not only do we finish the prayer, we supersize it! We have a beautiful prayer that revs us up to the pinnacle of the Our Father where we proclaim that the kingdom, the power, and the glory are God's now and forever. Before we say those words, the priest offers a powerful prayer for our peace and protection and reminds us of our hope in the resurrection. He says, 'Deliver us, Lord, we pray, from every evil, graciously grant peace in our days, that, by the help of your mercy, we may be always free from sin and safe from all distress, as we await the blessed hope and the coming of our Savior, Jesus Christ.'"

Talk about a barrier buster! Having the priest, who is acting as Jesus (*in persona Christi*), ask God to grant us peace and protect us from all anxiety is an amazing concept to fathom.

KEEPING IT TOGETHER: PRACTICAL WAYS OF FINDING YOUR PEACE

If we falter in our quest to find peace, we don't need to beat ourselves up. God has created us to be in relationship with him. Throughout the story of salvation, God's chosen people fail over and over to trust him. But God never abandoned the Israelites; rather, each time they lacked trust in him or abandoned him, he showed them he was forever faithful. He did this all the way to Calvary. God cherishes his children, and he will always lead us back to his heart.

So, what are some practical things we can do when we find ourselves doubting God's plan for our lives or when we struggle in trusting him completely? Well, when the barriers of doubt or fear threaten our peace, we must remember our purpose. We have been created for relationship: to know and love God and to share that love with others.

Here are some ways to break down the barriers to peace while strengthening your relationship with Christ:

Surrender your anxiety. Simply say: "Jesus, I trust in you; Jesus, I trust in you." Or, if you are struggling with trusting the Lord at that moment, ask Mary to help you trust her Son. She will always bring you to him.

Meditate on his Word. Spend a few moments each day in the Scriptures. Let God's promises become part of your daily life. Take comfort in knowing that God will fully satisfy our hearts now and forever. Here are a few suggestions to get you started: Psalm 16:11; John 6:45; John 7:37–38; Philippians 3:8–9.

Pray. Try carving out a daily prayer time. Designate a place to pray—perhaps a room, or a specific area in a room. Add a candle, some soft lighting, your favorite icon, a statue of the Blessed Mother, and so on. Make it a place where you feel comfortable— a place you long to be.

Serve others. Take your eyes off your own suffering by entering into a relationship with the poor, the lonely, or the elderly. Check to see if you parish has a ministry you can get involved in that serves those in need.

Listen. Set aside time each day for quietness. It is in the stillness that you can hear the voice of God. Take five minutes a day to unplug, log out, and disconnect. Simply rest in the presence of God.

Jesus is our peace. As a woman created to relate, you can tap into this divine peace right now. It doesn't matter if you are fighting cancer, battling depression, taking care of aging parents, sleep-deprived from tending to young children, or feeling as though you are under a heap of bills and will never see the light of day. God's peace has been promised to you since the beginning of creation. Just rest in him and let his peace fill your heart.

TOOLS FOR BUILDING YOUR RELATIONSHIPS
Scripture

In John 19:26 read what Jesus did when he saw his mother standing at the foot of the cross, and then read it again more slowly. Then read it for a third time, noting the words or insights that jump out at you. Write down those words and the thoughts you had about them.

Meditation

Just as Jesus trusted his Father in accepting the cross, so did Mary. She stood by Jesus lovingly with inconceivable sorrow. In your mind's eye, picture her at the foot of the cross.

Imagine yourself standing beside the three women at the foot of Jesus's cross. Speak to Jesus there, saying, "Jesus, I trust you."

QUESTIONS FOR REFLECTION AND DISCUSSION

1. Recall a time and place where you observed what seemed to be a chaotic and confusing situation. Perhaps it was final preparatory days before celebrating a wedding: so much to do, so little time. Or perhaps it was the days following the death of

a family member or close friend: selection of details for the funeral, logistics for family and friends coming from far away, and so on. Often these busy times are closely connected to life events. How did the people involved keep all the stuff of the moment loving, perhaps even happy? How could you prepare to keep Christ in the center of such a life event of your own?

2. Peace is not an absence of difficulty or pain, but a living *presence* that assures you of your safety and value despite sorrow or suffering. When have you experienced this kind of peace in your life? If you haven't had such an experience, what might you do to change this?

3. "Have no anxiety about anything, but *in everything* by prayer and supplication with thanksgiving let your requests be made know to God," writes St. Paul in Philippians 4:6 (emphasis added). Imagine St. Paul sitting next to you today, listening to you as you shared with him how difficult it is to pray with thanksgiving. Think of him asking you, "What in your *everything* are you struggling to give thanks to God for?" How would you answer? What do you hear Jesus (or St. Paul) saying to you about this? How might you pray differently?

4. When you attend Mass the next time, pay special attention to the fact that the Our Father contains a powerful request for peace. How could this realization change your heart when you pray the Our Father?

5. How has your trust in God grown through the merciful way he has acted in your life?

LIVING YOUR RELATIONAL GIFT

Option 1: Go to where you know Jesus would want you to be— with those who are not able to be at Mass. Call your parish and ask about the ministers who take Eucharist to the homebound. Arrange to go with one of the ministers on one of their visits to someone who is not able to attend Mass. Bringing the Body of Christ to those who are homebound is a visit from Jesus to the one who cannot come to him in the tabernacle. You bring the concern of the Church to those who cannot be active in the life of the parish.

Option 2: Recall a painful memory, a time when you "couldn't pray" and tears were your daily bread. How did that painful experience slowly subside? Tell yourself *your* own story about that time; perhaps write it down. Record what happened that destroyed your peace and crushed your spirit. Then explain how God brought you out of that experience of sorrow, led you to depend on relationship with him, and brought peace back to you. Keep the record for a time when you need to hear *your* story again.

CHAPTER NINE

Balancing the Relationship Between
Your Martha and Mary

Not even three seconds after I hit the send button to let people know about an upcoming event, my sister Sally e-mailed back, "Did you make a Facebook Evite yet?"

"Sally, Sally, Sally! What do you mean? Don't you know I just dashed off that last e-mail quickly so I could get to my cut-and-color appointment (ten minutes late), race to my fourteen-year-old's lacrosse game, leave early to make a beeline to the batting cages to pick up my son, get him something to eat, drop him off at home, throw in a load of whites, pick up my seventeen-year-old daughter from play practice, drive her to her babysitting job, pick up toilet paper and syrup at the grocery store, dash home to feed the dog, and sit down to frantically write an article that is due in... umm...thirty minutes!"

And all of this on a day that I promised myself I was going to let go of my inner "Martha" and connect with my inner "Mary"! How do you think that plan went for me? Yep, you guessed it. Martha trumped Mary, again, and that can be such a discouraging feeling—especially on days when I tell myself I am going to schedule time to just sit and pray.

A TALE OF TWO SISTERS

In case you are wondering who these two "inner" women living in my head are, rest assured, they don't truly live in my head;

the one thing is needful

rather, they are women I relate to from Scripture (one of them more than the other). In St. Luke's Gospel, when Jesus visits the home of the two sisters, Martha and Mary, in Bethany, Martha shows herself to be anxious and distracted while Mary keeps her eyes fixed upon the Lord.

> Now as they went on their way, he entered a village; and a woman named Martha received him into her house. And she had a sister called Mary, who sat at the Lord's feet and listened to his teaching. But Martha was distracted with much serving, and she went to him and said, "Lord, do you not care that my sister has left me to serve alone? Tell her then to help me." But the Lord answered her, "Martha, Martha, you are anxious and troubled about many things; one thing is needful. Mary has chosen the good portion, which shall not be taken away from her." (Luke 10:38–42)

If you are anything like me—a busy woman who finds it hard to say no to just one more project—chances are that you struggle to find that same balance between your active life and your prayer life.

When I find myself like Martha, overwhelmed by daily activities, I can easily beat myself up. But it gets worse. Truth be told, I like my inner Martha, busy though she may be. I am comfortable with her. Oftentimes, I welcome the distractions she brings, because when I sit with my inner Mary, I find myself fidgeting or wondering what I'm going to make for dinner, or lamenting over all of the things I could be getting done.

However, in these moments I hear God say: "Kelly, Kelly, you are anxious and troubled about many things." *Yep, Lord, you've got me pegged there.* As my heart settles, I know I just need to be with him, to sit in his presence. "One thing is needful," says the Lord (Luke 10:42).

In other words, I need not worry that I am fidgety or that my prayer life isn't good enough. I just need to be with Jesus. And while I'm with Jesus, there's no need to fret over the fact that beef stroganoff has entered my mind. I simply need to acknowledge it might be a great dinner option and go back to resting in him. Discipleship sometimes requires that tasks must wait while my relationship with God is nurtured.

When I feel like I'm not measuring up spiritually, I simply remember John 11:5— "Now Jesus loved Martha." This thought comforts me and gives me hope that, even in my busyness, the Lord loves me and will always work to ensure I focus on him. Sometimes I think Martha got kind of bad rap. What if no one had cooked the dinner or prepared the house for Jesus's coming? Who would have made him feel at home? What would they have had for dinner if Martha hadn't been in charge? Martha was a relational woman. She recognized the needs of others and went out of her way to take care of them.

I imagine that Jesus loved seeing Martha share her many virtues—among them her hospitality, kindness, and deep faith. While living out her vocation as a woman, she cared for and nurtured her family and friends, enhancing the relationships of those around her.

Jesus didn't chide Martha because she was hospitable. He simply challenged her to be less distracted. He pretty much said, "Martha, eyes on me." At that moment, I wonder if Martha put down the food she was preparing and wiped her brow. I can almost hear her saying: "You're right, Lord. I'm wearing myself down."

Not only was this a beautiful lesson for Martha, it seems to have spurred a desire in the disciples to want to know how they, too, could find that down time, how they could suspend their tasks and work on their relationship with God. In the very next chapter, St. Luke tells us that one of Jesus's disciples said to him, "Lord, teach us to pray." As a mom, I'm oh-so-familiar with this type of teaching. You teach a lesson to one child in earshot of the others who also need to learn that very lesson.

Jesus, the ultimate teacher, was successful in his lesson that day with all audiences. When we see Martha again, she proves that Jesus had impacted her faith. She greets Jesus on the road (again a beautiful act of hospitality) and says, "And even now I know whatever you ask from God, God will give you" (John 11:22). Can you picture the scene? I'm imagining Martha's eyes fixed on her Savior, her face radiant with trust. I can see Jesus smiling knowingly at the gracious woman who has served him so well. She goes on to say, "Yes, Lord: I believe that you are the Christ, the Son of God, he who is coming into the world" (John 11:27). Martha, a simple woman, has become an evangelizer. She has proclaimed Jesus as the Christ, the Messiah, the Savior of the world.

In his letter "On the Dignity and Vocation of Women" (*Mulieris Dignitatem*), St. John Paul II says: "This conversation with Martha is one of the most important in the Gospels. It appears Martha took to heart the lesson Jesus taught her; for, she professes him the Son of God and he in turn entrusts her as a "guardian of the Gospel message."[27] What a message of hope for all of us struggling to balance our lives!

BALANCE EQUALS PEACE

When do you feel like Martha? When are you most distracted from Jesus? For me it is when I am pulled in a too many different directions. For instance, one autumn I was scheduled to give a talk on how to keep your eyes fixed on Jesus and find balance in life. And wouldn't you know it, the weeks leading up to that talk were riddled with distractions! (God has a funny way of making us practice what we preach.) My daughter was starting college, I was beginning a national women's ministry, I was overseeing every detail of the largest student body ever enrolled in the Archbishop Harry J. Flynn Catechetical Institute where I was working, I had a full schedule of speaking engagements over the three months (and still had to write four of the talks), and I had multiple writing assignments with deadlines. And then there was that killer talk on balancing one's active and contemplative life! My life was a whirlwind.

When we find our lives out of balance, when we feel as though we are teetering on the edge of discord, agitation, and frustration, the reason is because we have let something, or someone, rob us of our peace.

Think about it. How many times has something happened at work, in your family, or in a relationship and you have stewed on it, playing the scenario over and over in your head, going through what you "shoulda" or "coulda" said or done? We've all had times when a lack of forgiveness keeps us preoccupied with bitterness and resentment. And what about our nonstop routines and schedules? How many times have you thought, *Why did I say yes to that project? What was I thinking?* For many of us, it feels like we have to pencil God into our daily planner.

That autumn when I felt pulled in multiple directions, I heeded the Lord's advice and made it a priority to spend more time with him in prayer morning and night. Though it was hard to juggle the demands of my schedule, I went to daily Mass and added an hour of Adoration to my day. At times, it was really hard, and I bargained with the Lord and said: "Lord, how about if I add just one weekday Mass? Will that do?" But in the recesses of my heart, I heard the Lord say, "Choose me over all things. Tasks and priorities will pass. But the good portion will not be taken from you."

When our lives feel scattered, distress and agitation can become a way of life. But God wants us to have balance in all areas of our life. His plan is for us to feel good emotionally, spiritually, and physically. He has created us to relate, and our relationship with him comes before all others. Only when we take the time to sit at his feet can we know his will for our lives. When we are spending time with him on a daily basis, we will come to know what our priorities should be and how we are called to spend our days on earth.

It's worth spending time with God, as Martha's sister Mary did. During our baptism, the Holy Spirit gave us divine life and we became God's children, called to share in the salvific mission of the Son to make disciples of all nations. In other words, we have been created for God's own purposes. In fact, Jesus tells us that, in him, *we can do all things*. In him, we can find balance in the chaotic autumns of our lives. But it takes discernment to know what things we *are called* to do.

LIVING YOUR GIFTS

From time to time, most of us ask the question: "What should I do, God?" The answer to this question can be found in the gifts freely given by the Holy Spirit to each baptized Christian. These gifts, called charisms, enable us to be a part of bringing others to salvation by relating to them where they are at in their journey.

A charism is a gift that achieves God's purpose. Charisms build up the body of Christ and give us the strength and power to evangelize. Charisms help others to know, love, and serve God. They are gifts given to each of us for the salvation of others. How beautifully relational that is!

What are your charisms? Do you have the gift of teaching? Can you sing? Do people tell you that your prayers for them have a powerful effect? Do others often look to you for encouraging words or for leadership? Do others feel welcome in your presence? If you're not sure, think about this: Have you ever known exactly what to do and exactly when to do it, but you didn't know why you knew those things? And I'm guessing the outcome might have been beyond anything you could have ever fathomed!

Working in your charism brings great joy. When you exercise your gifts, there is a sense that something is happening beyond your control, something awesome for the greater good. When you use your charisms, other people recognize your gifts and point them out to you, and you are both encouraged and inspired by their insights. If you are working in your charism, you will feel energized—you will feel like you are in your groove.

Do you know what your particular charisms are? If you don't, this can be easily remedied. Just pray to the Holy Spirit and ask him to reveal your gifts. One of the best tools I have found in helping me to recognize and live in my gifts is the Called and Gifted workshops offered by the Catherine of Siena Institute. If you are not familiar with the Catherine of Siena Institute, look

diabolos
devil - thrown apart — what's happening to us and our nation / our faith

me, devil wants us to be scattered

into what they offer with respect to gift discernment. For me, this workshop was life changing.

Another reason that we may not be working in our charisms can be seen in the story of Martha and Mary. While Martha certainly had the gift of hospitality, the Lord points out that she is just going through the motions. Focused on her to-do list, she is anxious and worried about many things. She's just too busy!

If we are anxious and worried about many things, we can't focus on what God has called us to do or how we are meant to use our gifts. This is a tactic of the one who does not want to see the kingdom of God flourish, the one who is the direct opposite of peace and love. Scattering our thoughts so we cannot concentrate on the things of God is diabolical; it is the work of the devil.

The word *diabolic* comes from the Greek word *diabolos* and means having qualities of the devil. In the Bible, *diabolos* is translated as "devil" over a thousand times. The word actually comes from two root words: *dia,* meaning "apart," and *ballein,* meaning "to throw."[28] It literally means to throw apart. That's what the devil wants to do. He is the force behind disconnection, disintegration, and alienation. The devil wants to shatter and scatter our lives, our relationships, our attention on the will of God, and our focus on doing that will. If we are focused on many other things, our eyes will be off Jesus and his divine will for our lives.

Picture Martha's life as a beautiful vase. When Martha was working in her charism and her eyes were on the Lord, she was whole and complete. Just as a vase is used to hold and keep flowers alive, so, too, Martha was designed to hold the beauty of the love of Jesus. But when she took her focus off Jesus and became preoccupied with the duties and responsibilities of life, she was no longer whole and complete. On the contrary, she was like a shattered vase, unable to display God's peace and joy.

Ah, but we can take great comfort from Martha's story. In Christ, our lives will not be scattered and broken. I mean it! He really über-counters anything that threatens to tear us apart. Even the diabolic plans of the devil cannot and will not throw us apart. Remember the meaning of *shalom*? We are whole and complete in the Lord. Nothing missing. Nothing broken. Created to relate, we are women who will find our "one peace" in Christ.

Balancing Your Spiritual Life

"We contribute to our own burnout when we do for others what others are called to do." This is a line I have used for years when giving seminars on how to run Bible studies or how to implement and grow a fruitful women's ministry in your parish—and it is so true! When we take on the work of others, we become fatigued and sometimes even bitter.

As women, I think our natural gifts of assisting, caring, and nurturing help us slide down this slippery slope of taking on too much. How many times have you heard yourself say, "I'll do it," or, "I've got it," and only moments later find yourself thinking, *Where am I going to find the time to do that?* It used to happen to me all the time until I learned what my gifts were and began equipping others to use theirs. This is another win-win-win situation. Burnout is never good for anyone. When a workload is shared, all of God's children have an opportunity to share their charisms. And no one has to play the role of a stressed-out, overburdened Martha.

In the story of Martha and Mary, each woman serves the Lord in a different way, according to their charisms. We could say that each of them represents different aspects of the spiritual life. Martha typifies the active life, honoring Christ by engaging in all her tasks, while Mary signifies the contemplative life. She shows her love for Christ by being still and listening to him.

My own active life consists of caring for my family as a wife and mother, directing a catechetical institute, and traveling the world sharing the Gospel. These important roles afford me opportunities to build holy relationships and share my faith. But as a child baptized into the family of God, perfecting my contemplative life is the goal. Like Martha, I need to be mindful of the busyness that defines my life. Amid all my callings, I need to pay attention to the voice of Jesus saying: "Kelly, only one thing is needed."

What is the one thing that is needed in your life? Are you taking time for it? Like many women, I live in a whirlwind of chaos, but I'm learning to take time for Jesus each day. I encourage you to do the same. Granted, it's not always doable to slip away to a daily Mass or to sit in front of the Blessed Sacrament. Mothers pretty much serve their families 24/7. Women in careers must sometimes jostle many schedules. Some women do both. But here's an idea: The next time you feel like your life is spinning out of control, take a quiet moment to close your eyes. Imagine yourself sitting at the feet of Jesus, as Mary did. Allow God to speak to your heart. Tell him your needs and ask for help in getting through the rest of the day. Know that God is with you and that he will give you the strength you need. Taking time for Jesus is the most important thing you can do. Trust me, you will see radical changes in your life when you do.

I think Martha got that; I really do. I think she learned that spending time with Jesus balanced her—because in John 12 we see her once again making supper, serving Jesus, and caring for her family, yet she is no longer anxious. Her life is no longer scattered—she is joyfully working in her gifts with Jesus before her.

As I close this chapter, I'd like to share a visual that correlates perfectly with the story of Mary and Martha: M&Ms. Yes, I'm using chocolate to teach about the things of God. M&Ms are the perfect balance of chocolate and candy coating. The best part of the M&M is the center, the rich chocolate morsel. Think of that center as the contemplative life—the soft, sweet interior of soul, the place where God resides. The outer candy coating is what everybody sees. It is the colorful, protective exterior and in this scenario, our active life. Though both of these confectionary attributes are necessary to create the perfect sweet that melts in your mouth (not in your hands), it is reaching that sweet center that is the ultimate goal.

So, the next time you pick up an M&M, remember the story of Martha and Mary. Don't forget that busy Martha learned to balance her outer good works with the inner transformation of her spirit. Created to relate to her Lord, she listened to him, changed her ways, and joyfully used her gifts to serve him.

Today, use your "chocolate fix" as an opportunity to ask the Lord to help you find that perfect balance. Treat yourself to a small bag of M&Ms. Every time you eat an M&M, simply say, "Lord, give me balance as I strive to do your will today." (Think of the prayers and graces if you eat the whole bag!)

Tools for Building Your Relationships
Scripture

In John 14:27 read how Jesus leaves us his peace, and then read it again, more slowly. Then read it for a third time, noting the words or insights that jump out at you. Write down those words and the thoughts you had about them.

Meditation

Prayerfully imagine yourself as a third sister in the house with Martha and Mary when Jesus came to visit them. Would you be sitting at Jesus's feet with Mary or helping Martha in the kitchen? Imagine Jesus greeting you by name. What does say to you?

QUESTIONS FOR REFLECTION AND DISCUSSION

1. Have you ever had as frantic a day, filled with tasks and errands tumbling on top of each other, such as the one described at the beginning of this chapter? To avoid being disconnected spiritually on such a day, what reminders can you use to keep focused on Jesus? How about a statue of the Sacred Heart in your home, or a rosary in your car? Write down what you can do to focus your day and keep your "eyes on Jesus."

2. What are the "many things" you are worried about? Select the top five and list them. Next to each one, write one of two words: "Jesus" or "me." If the worry is about what might happen to you, write "me." If the worry is about how you can take care of this as Jesus would want you to, write "Jesus." Which of the "Jesus" worries have you asked him to help you with? Which of the "me" worries can you do anything about without the help of Jesus? Share with Jesus how solutions to these worries can help intensify your relationship with him. If you are studying this book in a group, pick one worry and share what you asked Jesus to do about it with the other participants.

3. List a few of your friends. Beside each name, write each one's gifts (plural—everyone has more than one gift). Under each gift write a word or two signifying when and how you became

aware of those gifts. Now write your name. Beside your name, write your gifts (plural). Under your gifts write a word signifying when and how you knew you had them. How have you used them for Jesus? Ask him to show you how he would like you to use them in the future, and write down his answer.

4. Think about an event, a day, or an experience when you lost track of time. Perhaps you were experiencing so much joy in your activities and in the friends and family with you that time flew by. Charisms build the kingdom, and that building is acted out *in relationships*. What current relationships do you have where you can continue to use your charisms for the kingdom?

5. Do you know anyone you could encourage to use his or her charisms for the kingdom? How could you start that encouragement? And when?

Living Your Relational Gift

Option 1: Who are three people you will *definitely* come in contact with this week? In your mind, create a compliment for each one, something that calls attention to one of that individual's gifts in a specific encounter where the two of you were present. Deliver that compliment when you come in contact with each of your three choices this week. After they respond, tell them you'll spend a specific time in prayer for them.

Option 2: Recall a time when you felt "thrown apart," either in your own spiritual life, your family, your career, your vocation, or some other aspect of your life. You made your way through the "forces of disconnection, disintegration, and alienation," and you are here reading this book and sharing your victories in relationships with others, with Jesus. Thank Jesus for the gift of those in relationship with you who helped you regain his peace.

CHAPTER TEN

Peace and Joy in God's Design

Recently, a priest I've known for years reminded me of my college days. Now, if you knew me in college, this would be the point where you'd be saying, "All right! Finally, this book is getting interesting!" Sorry to burst your bubble, but it wasn't the shenanigans of my youth he reminded me of—it was the days and nights I spent trying to understand St. Thomas Aquinas. Just a quick disclaimer here, lest you think for one minute that I had some great grasp of my faith back then or that I was some type of theology buff, I didn't and I wasn't. I was taking a course called "History of Catholic Thought—Part I" because I needed three theology credits to graduate, and after twelve years of Catholic school, this course sounded simple enough not to interfere with my senior year fun. Was that assumption ever wrong!

The class was a requirement for seminarians, so it consisted of fifteen brilliant men eager to know the intricacies of their faith and ten others just eager to graduate. In the class, we walked through the early Church and covered every aspect of every heresy the early Christians encountered. It was one of the toughest college classes I had ever taken (and I was pre-med, a biology major with a focus on genetics, minoring in chemistry and psychology). Needless to say, I was thrilled at the end of the semester when the class was over and I had all the theology credits I needed to graduate.

One seminarian, however, decided to practice his "Catholic guilt" tactics to get me to sign up for "History of Catholic Thought—Part II," a class I did not need to take at all. He would say things like, "How can you only get half a history?" and, "It will bother you for the rest of your life that you never learned the second half of the history of the Church," and, "Quitting now is like leaving a nail-biting movie ten minutes before the end." Soon he had all his seminarian buddies chiming in too, and before I knew it, I caved and signed up for Part II. The second semester, the class was much smaller. It now consisted of sixteen students, and only one was a woman. Guess who?

My "fun" elective class that last semester of my senior year of college was spent studying the *Summa Theologica*. While everyone else was taking pottery, or weight-lifting, or bowling, or music appreciation (referred to by some of my fellow students as "clapping for credit"), I was trying to wrap my brain around the profound works of St. Thomas Aquinas. Did I know how to have a good time, or what? So, when Fr. Steven reminded of my college years, this was the class that came to mind.

THE PERFECT DIVINE HELPER

Fr. Steven and I were talking about the story of creation in Genesis 2. We were discussing the hierarchy of creation: how woman wasn't created *second*, she was created *last*. Fr. Steven referenced a concept found many times in the *Summa*. He said, "That which is last in the order of execution is first in the order of intention."[29]

Right about now, you might be thinking: *What in the world does that mean?*

In plain language, it means that we can gain insight into the intentions of God by looking at how he creates—in particular looking at what he creates last. Remember Eve? She was the last in the story of creation to be fashioned by the hand of God, "built" from the "finer stuff." She comes to life *after* everything else is made; after God created the heavens and the earth, after the trees were firmly rooted and filled with fruit, after the seas were brimming with fish, after the birds were singing and all manner of animals were roaming through the Garden of Eden. She takes her first breath *after* she is formed from Adam's rib.

Yes, Eve is fashioned last. But her creation gives us a glimpse into the mind and heart of our glorious God. Eve completes God's *intention* to "make man in our image, after our likeness" (Genesis 1:26). The creation of Eve completes the mirror image of the Trinity.

Without Eve, Adam doesn't make sense. It is Eve who reveals that we are created for relationship. This is why when Adam sees her he cries out, "This at last is bone of my bones and flesh of my flesh" (Genesis 2:23). Adam now realizes that he, too, has been created for relationship; it took seeing Eve, the one "built" (*binah*) to be his "divine helper" (*ezer*) to open his eyes and recognize this (voilà!). In Eve, Adam recognized "an equal, a person like himself whom he could love. That is, he saw someone to whom he could give himself completely and who could receive and reciprocate his gift to form a union that would fulfill the very meaning of their existence."[30]

In Vatican II's "Pastoral Constitution on the Church in the Modern World," (*Gaudium et Spes*), we read these enlightening words:

> Eve complements Adam perfectly and in turn they reflect the relationship of the Most Holy Trinity, who is

a communion, who is a perfect self-giving and selfless receiving relationship of love.[31]

From the very beginning, God wanted us to be in communion with one another. We were never meant to live solitary lives, alone and disconnected from the kingdom of God. We were created to relate, to care for one another, and to travel this journey together.

The intuitive woman knows, on a deep and profound level, how to share the selfless love of Christ. Most mothers don't think twice about washing mountains of clothes, fixing countless meals, or caring for a sick child in the middle of the night. We do these things out of love. In our friendships, we don't mind talking with a friend in need, sometimes for hours at a time. Though many of us have the gift of gab, we can be incredibly good listeners, too. And if we aren't having a "Martha" day, distracted with our schedules and routines, we listen well and respond faithfully.

As I reflect upon the great women I have known in my life, they have all been self-givers. My mother, grandmother, and Auntie Lani each exemplified selflessness. I think of Carol Marquardt and the way she cared for her dying husband. I think of the women I've met in my ministry work traveling the country—teachers, nurses, nuns, receptionists, child-care givers, Bible study leaders, conference coordinators, countless volunteers, and hardworking moms. These amazing women are in the trenches of faith each day, tirelessly serving and teaching others about Christ. And I can't forget the great female saints who have played such a huge role in my spiritual journey: St. Mary Magdalene, Blessed Mother Teresa, St. Thérèse of Lisieux, St. Catherine of Siena, and Sts. Elizabeth and Martha, just to name just a few.

God has woven these relationships throughout my life. Each relationship I've known is a thread in God's hand, intertwined with mine in a tapestry of love. God has given each strand a different color and texture, according to the gifts he's given each of us. It's a design that reflects the light of God, a masterpiece to be cherished.

In this woven design of life is a subtle element connecting the many colors and hues, a golden thread that is laced throughout. This luminous thread transfigures the tapestry from mere art to dazzling masterpiece. It's the light of Mary, our Blessed Mother. God has given her a special place in his design for women. He has granted her "the fullness of perfection of what is characteristic of woman, of what is feminine" (*Mulieris Dignitatem, 5*)

From the beginning, she was destined to be *Theotokos*, the Mother of God. Mary is *the image of the Divine choice of every creature*, a choice which was made from eternity, and was totally free, mysterious, and loving: "In the mystery of Christ she is present even 'before the creation of the world,' as the one whom the Father 'has chosen' *as Mother* of his Son in the Incarnation. And, what is more, together with the Father, the Son has chosen her, entrusting her eternally to the Spirit of holiness" (5, 6).

GOD'S MASTERPIECE
Like Eve, Mary was fashioned for God's holy purpose; she was *built* from the *finest* things: humility, trust, and purity of heart. Blessed among women, she was given a great measure of *binah*. God choose her and poured into her the fullness of his love and life. He made her "full of grace" (*kécharitôménê*). Mary is God's masterpiece!

Think about it: if you set out to paint a picture, you begin with an image. In your mind, you know exactly what you want to paint. You create your to-do list: you determine the size of your masterpiece, build the frame, lay the canvas, and choose the paint, colors, and brushes. You begin to prepare the canvas, chalk the outline, apply the pale under-painting, and add the mid-tones and shadows until the picture starts to emerge. Then you work, adding important details, until the masterpiece is finished. God, the ultimate artist, creates in the same way.[4] He has the intention of his masterpiece in mind long before he begins to create, and God's most perfect human creation, his masterpiece, is Mary.

Jesus.

Though we cannot totally comprehend many of the works of God, for his thoughts are not our thoughts and his ways are not our ways (see Isaiah 55:8), this is one we can grasp. Simply put, if you were God and you were going to create your mother, wouldn't you make her perfect? She is the mother of the One who will save all of humanity through his passion, death, and resurrection. I don't know about you, but if I were God, I would absolutely make the mother of my only begotten Son my masterpiece!

Mary provided a way for Christ to assume our humanity. Through Mary's obedience to God's plan, Christ became one of us, our friend, brother, healer, and savior. Mary, created without sin, opened the door for us to have a deep and personal relationship with Christ. Our Blessed Mother helped us discover our purpose, our dignity, our calling to be in communion with one another.

As a graduation gift, my daughter's favorite religion teacher made her an icon. It was a beautiful work of art. Talk about a God-given gift! What struck me most about the icon was that it captured the angel Gabriel waiting for Mary's reply. I found myself asking: What was it like for all of heaven to know that the salvation of the world rested on the response of this young girl?

Though Mary may not have understood the "bigness" of God's plan she responded with unwavering trust in her God. Mary's every word and every deed calls us to remember the importance of knowing, serving, and loving God.

THE FIRST EVANGELIST

Through Mary's perfect surrendering to the divine will, through her living perfectly God's plan for her life, through her living perfectly her vocation as woman, the salvation of the world came to be in Christ Jesus. This was God's plan in creating Mary without sin. It was his plan from the beginning for her to be the Mother of the Son of God, and it was his plan that through her the Son of God could assume our human nature to accomplish our salvation in it.

Mary shows us that the word "yes" holds great power. Every action, every word, every thought of Mary is perfectly conformed to the will of God. Her relationship with God was the center of her life. The unbreakable bond she shares with Jesus is the bond that draws her into relationship with others.

Mary not only bears Christ, she shares him with the world. From the moment she goes in haste to Elizabeth, to her journey on a donkey to Bethlehem, to the wedding feast in Cana, Mary shares Jesus with everyone she encounters. At the Visitation, when Elizabeth is in need, Mary brings her Jesus. Remember, Elizabeth is old, has been barren, and is living off in the hills. Yet Mary goes to her. At the Incarnation, she brings Jesus into the world that needs him desperately. In a manger, the Savior of the world is born through her. And at the wedding in Cana, Mary shows the

world that Jesus will take care of our every need. All we need do
is trust him.

Mary is the first evangelist. Because she knew him, loved him,
and served him, she was able to share Jesus with others. Her entire
life was a *lectio divina*, a meditation on the Word of God. Even in
her busiest moments as a wife, mother, friend, cousin, Mary kept
her eyes on Jesus, and rested in him. She knew the *good portion*!

As a mother, every ounce of my energy was spent on providing
for the needs of my children when they were babies. But it was
in those crazy, sleep-deprived days and nights that I found my
greatest joy. I can easily remember those moments when my first
child drifted off to sleep in my arms. I couldn't stop looking at
her. I couldn't stop lightly kissing her face. I remember thinking,
"I can't believe I can love this much." It was this way with all
three of my children. This must have been what Mary experienced every time she looked at *her* son. Her heart must have been
bursting with love.

Mary's surrender takes her to the cross. But she is not alone.
She is surrounded by friends who stand with her. No doubt the
prophetic words of wise old Simeon at the Presentation of Jesus
are echoing in the Blessed Mother's head, "And a sword will
pierce through your own soul also" (Luke 2:35). But even in the
most intense pain, there is comfort in the arms of another. With
the Blessed Mother at the foot of the cross was Mary Magdalene,
Mary, the wife of Clopas, and John, the disciple whom Jesus loved.
I imagine that, throughout the whole horrific ordeal, the four of
them took turns holding each other up, physically and emotionally. As they heard the sounds of their Savior being scourged, as
they watched their Messiah fall under the weight of the cross,

as they witnessed nails pounded into the hands and feet of their Lord, and as their God breathed his last, I can see each of them encouraging the others to persevere in their plight to be with Jesus. Taking turns, each of them has become a "they" for the others, bringing them close to Christ in their greatest suffering.

MARY ACHIEVES PERFECTLY WHAT EVE WAS BUILT FOR

Every word of Mary's is a word of surrender, from her words at the annunciation (see Luke1:38) to her last recorded words in Sacred Scripture at the wedding in Cana: "Do whatever he tells you" (John 2:5). Mary's words are said with pure humility, and because of that, they carry great authority.

Imagine if you were a servant at the wedding in Cana. Perhaps you don't even know Jesus; maybe you've seen Mary around Nazareth, and suddenly she comes up to you and says, "Do whatever he tells you."

Those are pretty powerful words. I imagine my response would be a quick and obedient, "Yes, ma'am."

Let's take a look at why her words at Cana are so meaningful:

First, Mary intuitively recognized human need. She knew that the wine was running out and that the family would be embarrassed. Created to relate to others, Mary wanted to aid those in need. Though the circumstances looked dire, she knew her Son was capable of a miracle. So many years earlier, she had heard the angel say: "Nothing shall be impossible for God."

Second, in ordering the servants to follow whatever Jesus commands, Mary is, in her way, evangelizing. When she says: "Do whatever he tells you," she is saying in essence: "Follow him. He is the Way, the Truth and the Life." All these years later, we are still following her lead. Every time we tell another person about

Jesus, we are saying: "Follow him.... Do whatever he tells you....
Your prayers will be answered in the most wondrous way."

Third, in saying this, Mary is opening the door for Jesus to
begin his active public ministry. She is starting him on the road
to Calvary. She is opening herself up to the greatest suffering,
sorrow, and pain that any woman has ever experienced. She
suffered greatly because she loved her Son so deeply. The more we
love someone, the more pain we feel when they suffer. Think of
those nights spent wiping the tears of a teen who has just had her
heart broken, or the hours spent comforting a close friend who
just received a bad report from the doctor. In those times you can
literally ache for another. Mary's love for her Divine Son was the
most perfect of human love, and therefore, her sufferings during
his suffering had to have been magnified; yet on that festive day
in Cana, she still surrenders to the will of God...and sets Jesus on
the road to Calvary.

Mary's surrender is beautifully captured in Michelangelo's *Pieta*.
In this world-famous work, the body of Jesus lays in the arms
of his grieving mother after the crucifixion. I remember standing
before this statue in St. Peter's Basilica in Vatican City with my
daughter Annika. Though surrounded by thousands of bustling
tourists, the two of us were completely drawn into the moment
Michelangelo set out to capture. It was as if time stood still as
we gazed upon the crucified Jesus cradled in his loving mother's
arms. Now, I love the Blessed Mother, and standing there with my
daughter looking into Mary's sorrowful face, and imagining what
it must have been like for her to hold her son's dead body in her
arms hit me like a ton of bricks. I ached for her. Michelangelo had
succeeded. He had relayed a powerful message, and through his

gift as an artist, he had brought me closer to Christ. While there is so much beauty and symbolism wrapped up in the *Pieta*, there was one feature that really captured my heart. In his sculpture, Michelangelo has carved an element as profound as it is subtle. If you look at Mary's left hand, which is barely visible, you see it is lying open—a symbol of surrender to God. By this simple gesture, Michelangelo has shown the world that Mary's entire life is a *fiat*. Mary always says yes to the will of God.

As a young girl Mary told the angel: "Be it done unto me." But this time in Cana, a woman who has raised the Son of God for thirty years now proclaims that God has, and will always be, faithful to his people. With great authority she says: "Do whatever he tells you." She is letting go of her boy. In doing so, she is stepping into a brand-new relationship with Jesus. No longer can she be the exclusive mother of Jesus. By sharing her Son, she is opening up her motherly heart to all. And at the foot of the cross, this will be firmly established as Jesus shares his mother with all of us. In fact, when he does this, he even refers to her as "woman" to trigger our thoughts of the first woman, Eve (*Chavah*, which means "Mother of All Life" in Hebrew).

> When Jesus saw his mother, and the disciple whom he loved standing near, he said to his mother, 'Woman, behold, your son!' Then he said to the disciple, 'Behold, your mother!' And from that hour the disciple took her to his own home. (John 19:26–28)

Today Mary relates to us as she related to all the folks who attended that wedding in Cana. Mercifully. Tenderly. Authoritatively. As she lived out her vocation as a woman, drawing others to her Son, she reminds us how much we need a Savior.

In fact, Jesus's reply to her is a beautiful reminder that she was fulfilling her vocation perfectly. He addressed her as "Woman" (see John 2:4). This is not a put down, nor is Jesus being rude. Rather, as we just learned he would again do from the cross, Jesus is connecting Mary to the first pinnacle of God's creation, Eve. Yet where the woman Eve fell in the garden, Mary has risen in her "yes' at the Annunciation, in her going in haste to Elizabeth in the Visitation, in the birth of her Son in Bethlehem, at a wedding feast in Cana, and in every other aspect of her life.

Mary is the *perfect* pinnacle, the masterpiece of God's creation, a bright light in the tapestry of God's love. Through her surrender to the Divine Will, Mary achieves perfectly that for which Eve was created. Mary *is* the perfect Divine Helper, bringing us into relationship—a divine relationship with the Father, Son, and Holy Spirit.

LIVING IN THE PERFECT PEACE WITH THE GREATEST JOY

The final song at the fiftieth anniversary Mass of my grandparents and the celebration of my First Communion was a song my Auntie Lani taught to all twenty-two of her nieces and nephews. Lani had this wonderful idea of having us all stand up and surprise our grandparents at the end of Mass by singing this song. Being that the year was 1977, it might have been the first-ever flash mob. (So, yes, you can thank my family for that little invention.) The only words I remember are: "Peace, joy, and happiness be yours, and fullness of life." After fifty years of marriage, eight children, twenty-two grandchildren, and a large loving family, I'd say my grandma and grandpa achieved that.

As I think about that song, I'm wishing you, my dear sister in Christ, the peace, joy, and happiness of the Lord. So, at the close of this book, I'm inviting you to believe that you are made in the image and likeness of God. It's a radical thought, I know, but the Lord of the universe longs to be in relationship with you. He thirsts for you.

When we receive his love as gift, we can begin to embrace God's design for our lives. And what is that design? That our lives would be woven together in relationships of love.

If you seek true happiness, then look deeply into the faces of the folks who fill your home, your workplace, and your church. Look into the eyes of the strangers you meet at your child's school, the dentist office, or as you walk through your neighborhood. Find the presence of Christ in the ordinary, everyday relationships of life. Close your eyes and know that you share a special, mystical, miraculous relationship with the saints and angels in heaven.

The people you see each day will lead you into deeper communion with your God. They will strengthen you to know him, serve him, and proclaim him. In them, Christ's word will come alive, and you will know true joy.

You have been created to relate. You are a part of a radical design, a shimmering thread in Gods tapestry of relationship. Go out and dazzle the world.

TOOLS FOR BUILDING YOUR RELATIONSHIPS
Scripture
Read Mary's response to the angel Gabriel in Luke 1:38, and then read it again, more slowly. Then read it for a third time, noting the words or insights that jump out at you. Write down those words and the thoughts you had about them.

Meditation
In quiet prayer, imagine yourself sitting in your most comfortable reading chair. An angel from God comes to you and says: "You,

dear woman, have been created for a very specific purpose. Will you surrender your will and plans for your life into God's hands? Will you listen to and follow the promptings of the Holy Spirit? Will you choose every day to be a faithful disciple of Jesus, the Son of God? This is his desire for you."

What is your response? *yes! Now show me please...*

QUESTIONS FOR REFLECTION AND DISCUSSION

1. Think about the sacrament of marriage. What conditions are meant to be present in this loving relationship? Mary's loving relationship with God and Christ's loving relationship with his Church have these same conditions. Can you identify those conditions in what we know of Mary's life from Scripture? What ways do these conditions reveal themselves in your personal relationship with Jesus?

2. Your loving relationship with God is the source of your loving relationship with others. When was your first *fiat* to the will of God—the first time you said, "Let it be done to me?" How much sacrifice of your own will was (and still is) involved?

3. The Son of God received his human nature through Mary. As our spiritual mother, Mary wants to bring us to birth in Jesus Christ, too. How does your relationship with Mary deepen your relationship with God? How does Mary help you bring the Gospel to others?

4. Mary shows us the purpose and dignity of humanity because Mary is focused completely on the will of God. Mary's being is in relationship to the three Persons of the Trinity. Consider how you relate to the three Persons of the Trinity. How do you speak to the Father? How do you listen to the Holy Spirit? How is the Son being born in your spiritual life? How would

you express the relationship you have with the three Persons to someone else?

5. Mary's first evangelical encounter, her visit with Elizabeth, is a song of joy, the Magnificat. Your song of joy in your relationship with the Lord is your shimmering thread in the tapestry of God's salvation. Reflect on the many relationships this thread weaves together into God's tapestry in history. How might this inspire you to relate differently to each person in your life now? How can your current relationships be an expression of your peace and joy in God's design?

LIVING YOUR RELATIONAL GIFT

Option 1: Every day for a week, keep a list of the joys given to you by God, both physical and spiritual. It should be a long list, if you watch attentively through each day. At the end of the week, count them all and compose your own Magnificat, incorporating all of them, from the most important to the least important. Take the prayer to your parish church, and read it aloud (but not *too* loudly) before the tabernacle.

Option 2: As you think about your many relationships, which individuals are you praying for? Does your prayer for them involve their response to the Gospel? When you think of your less personal relationships (familiar store clerks, the people who help you care for your car, clean your clothes, manicure your lawn, help you with housekeeping, or deliver your mail), who are you compelled to pray for? We are in relationships all day long. Surrender all your relational encounters on a chosen day this week. Offer a silent prayer for each encounter, and ask Jesus to bless each one with peace and joy in his design.

NOTES

1. Reconciliation and Penance, 16.
2. Reconciliation and Penance, 10.
3. See *Miracle* (2004), IMDb Quotes, http://www.imdb.com/title/tt0349825/trivia?tab=qt&ref_=tt_trv_qu.
4. G.K. Chesterton, *Orthodoxy* (New York: Dover, 2004), p. 113.
5. John Paul II, "Speech of the Holy Father Pope John Paul II Meeting with Ecclesial Movements and New Communities," http://www.vatican.va/holy_father/john_paul_ii/speeches/1998/may/documents/hf_jp-ii_spe_19980530_riflessioni_en.html.
6. Cheryl Hauer, "Mary: A First-century Jewish Woman," Bridges for Peace, http://www.bridgesforpeace.com/teaching-letter/article/mary-a-first-century-jewish-woman/ (accessed July 18, 2014).
7. Deborah Savage, "The Nature of Woman in Relation to Man: Genesis 1 and Genesis 2 through the Lens of the Metaphysical Anthropology of St. Thomas Aquinas," *Logos*, Winter 2014, p. 12.
8. Savage, p. 12.
9. Savage, p. 13.
10. Savage, p. 13.
11. Savage, p. 13.
12. Hauer.
13. *Evangelii Gaudium*, 103.
14. "Ten Reasons Why Men Lead and Women Follow," Lloydian Aspects, http://www.lloydianaspects.co.uk/dance/menlead.html.
15. Benedict XVI, Homily, St. Peter's Square, April 24, 2005, http://www.vatican.va/holy_father/benedict_xvi/homilies/documents/hf_ben-xvi_hom_20050424_inizio-pontificato_en.html.
16. *Evangelii Gaudium*, 28.
17. *Evangelii Gaudium*, 142.
18. *Evangelii Gaudium*, 131.
19. Madeleine L'Engle, *Walking on Water: Reflections on Faith and Art* (Wheaton, Ill.: Harold Shaw, 1980), p. 122.
20. Cardinal Dolan, Twitter , June 27, 2012, https://twitter.com/CardinalDolan/status/218045220133154817.
21. LaVonne Neff, *A Life for God: The Mother Teresa Treasury* (London: Fount, 1996), http://jameslau88.com/mother_teresa_on_blessed_are_you_among_women.html.
22. *Catechesi Tradendae*.

23. *Salvifici Doloris*, 5.
24. Stuart Wetland, "A Primer on Peace," http://www.catholic.com/magazine/articles/a-primer-on-peace (accessed July 18, 2014).
25. "Baltimore Catechism No. 1," question 6, http://www.sacred-texts.com/chr/balt/balt1.htm.
26. Jacques Philippe, *Searching for and Maintaining Peace: A Small Treatise on Peace of Heart* (New York: Alba, 2002), p. 97.
27. *Mulieris Dignitatem*, 15.
28. "Diablos," Strong's Concordance, Bible Hub, http://biblehub.com/greek/1228.htm.
29. St. Thomas Aquinas, *Summa Theologica*, I-II Q.1, a.1, ob.1.
30. Mary Healy, *Men and Women Are from Eden* (Cincinnati, Ohio: Servant, 2005), p. 15.
31. *Gaudium et Spes*, 24.

Two Sisters Ministries

- charisms, talents, gifts
- spiritual life - health
- comm/
- punctuality

ABOUT THE AUTHOR

Kelly Wahlquist has a B.S. in biology with an emphasis on genetics from St. Mary's University and a B.A. in nursing from the College of St. Catherine. She left her nursing career to work full-time with Jeff Cavins in 2005. For five years, Kelly was the director of community relations for the Great Adventure Catholic Bible Study, and she is currently the assistant director of the Archbishop Harry J. Flynn Catechetical Institute, serving the Archdiocese of St. Paul and Minneapolis. She helped to create and implement this institute, which educates and equips the laity in the Catholic faith. For the past three years she has traveled extensively to Catholic conferences, where she is often the keynote speaker. This is her first book.